Evaluation in Contexts of Fragility, Conflict and Violence

Guidance from Global Evaluation Practitioners

Edited by

Hur Hassnain

Lauren Kelly

Simona Somma

Exeter, United Kingdom
Email: ideascoordinator@gmail.com

Citation: Hur Hassnain, Lauren Kelly and Simona Somma, eds. 2021. *Evaluation in Contexts of Fragility, Conflict and Violence: Guidance from Global Evaluation Practitioners*. Exeter, UK: IDEAS.

ISBN (paper): 978-1-9999329-5-4
ISBN (electronic): 978-9999329-6-1

Cover artwork: Tatsunori Kano (https://www.tatsunorikano.com/), mixed technique on canvas. Used with permission.
Cover design and interior layout: Nita Congress, www.behance.net/nitacongress

ENDORSEMENTS FOR
Evaluation in Contexts of Fragility, Conflict and Violence: Guidance from Global Evaluation Practitioners

"At least one-quarter of the world's population lives in zones affected by conflict, and almost all organizations working in international development must adapt many of their programs to the multiple challenges resulting from conflict. Despite this, the evaluation community has struggled to find ways to systematically assess how programs are affected by the multiple causes and consequences of these conflicts. *Evaluation in Contexts of Fragility, Conflict and Violence: Guidance from Global Evaluation Practitioners* offers practical step-by-step guidance on how to adapt the evaluation toolkit to the dramatically different contexts in which projects and programs operate in conflict zones. The approach is pragmatic, recognizing the many practical and ethical challenges facing evaluations in conflict zones, easy to follow and comprehensive. It also includes a wealth of case studies drawn from the in-the-trenches experience of seasoned evaluators. The guide also addresses two cutting-edge themes: the exciting contributions that big data, particularly geospatial analysis (satellites and drones), can offer in dangerous and inaccessible zones; and the need to apply a complexity framework to understand the multiple political, economic and sociocultural factors affecting how programs operate. The wealth of examples from the field, combined with the extensive review of applicable evaluation methods will be found invaluable by both new and experienced evaluators".

Michael Bamberger,
Development Evaluation Consultant

"This book is essential for all evaluators, especially, I believe, young and emerging evaluators who constitute the majority of the evaluation community members in the Global South, where this book is most relevant given the number of countries there that suffer from fragility, conflict and violence. I commend the generosity of all the authors for sharing their experience, hard work and lessons learned in this timely and vital book".

Khalil Bitar, Chair,
EvalYouth

"I encourage development practitioners to read this guidance. Fragility and conflict are among the most serious hurdles to achieving the 2030 Agenda and the Sustainable Development Goals. Evaluations can play a great role in promoting accountability and learning under fragility and conflict conditions. In order to be useful, evaluations need to be valid in the first place. For an evaluation to be valid in a fragile context, it is often insufficient to transpose the approach and methodology that would have been used in a different context. This guidance is a useful tool to orient evaluation specialists to enhance the validity of their findings, conclusions and recommendations, while respecting the situation of people in policymaking roles and affected by conflicts on the ground".

Fabrizio Felloni, Deputy Director and Officer in Charge,
Independent Office of Evaluation, International Fund for Agricultural Development

"Thinking around evaluations in fragile and conflict-affected situations is constantly evolving, and important new material and guiding literature can be difficult to keep up with. By having a guide that sets out the key aspects of the evaluation process that evaluators – and those commissioning evaluations – need to address is a valuable contribution to the sector. We look forward to using this guide in our own work and encourage others to make use of it too".

Tom Gillhespy, Principal Consultant,
Fragile and Conflict-Affected Settings Practice, Itad

"COVID-19 taught many lessons to the world including the greater value of learning from our own acts and from others for making better decisions to save people's lives. Evidence has been more essential in conflict and pandemic situations, and therefore this book is a great resource. The Asia Pacific Evaluation Association will ensure that the book will be disseminated in the region for use by practitioners".

Asela Kalugampitiya, President, Asia Pacific Evaluation Association, and
Secretariat, Global Parliamentarians Forum for Evaluation

"Fragility, conflict and violence – countries are increasingly prone to each of these conditions in an era of global pandemics and stark inequities. These conditions are complex, neither easy to address programmatically nor to evaluate. Every aspect of evaluation in these contexts brings its challenges – from identifying and accessing affected groups, understanding power dynamics, confronting fear and suspicion, collecting data in unsafe environments, and so forth. Therefore, this how-to book on evaluating in fragile, conflict and violent contexts is so important. Produced through a collaborative effort, it goes step by step through the evaluation process specifically applied to these contexts. I think it is particularly useful in offering web links throughout each section for those who want to go more deeply into topics, as well as in providing case studies and tips. I highly recommend it".

Linda Morra Imas, Co-Creator and Former Director,
International Program for Development Evaluation Training

"High-quality evaluation in fragile and humanitarian situations has become even more important today as we witness the entire world being gripped by one crisis or another. Whether it is human-engineered conflicts or climate crises, resources are scarce, and needs are high. In this context, it is even more important to know what works, how and why to mitigate the adverse consequences of crises. This handbook is an important, useful book to produce good-quality evidence while making real-world choices along the way about costs, data, rigour and methods. I recommend it for practitioners".

Jyotsna Puri, Director of Environment, Climate, Gender and Social Inclusion Division
International Fund for Agricultural Development

"In times of crisis, it is even more important for evaluation to do no harm and to do maximum good. Contexts of fragility, conflict and violence mean that evaluation needs to be done differently in order to be useful, valid, ethical and feasible. This timely guidance brings together hard-won lessons from individuals and organizations that have been doing evaluations in these difficult contexts over many years. This book provides useful advice from the early stages of understanding power and conflict to the final stages of reporting findings, with practical information about choosing methods and protecting staff and communities. The book has even wider relevance now as all countries deal with the crisis of the global pandemic and its implications for the types of interventions that are needed, the types of evaluations that are needed and the constraints on using traditional evaluation methods".

Patricia Rogers, Chief Executive Officer
BetterEvaluation

"The Decade for Action is here and there is no time to lose. This book, which results from an inspiring collaborative effort, is a valuable tool to nourish meaningful evaluation practice, strengthening our knowledge, skills, values and attitudes for acting effectively and ethically under risk, pressure and danger. I invite all International Organization for Cooperation in Evaluation member Voluntary Organizations for Professional Evaluation to disseminate and promote the use of this book, to ensure that evaluators are better equipped for the future and that evaluation practice strengthens its relevance and transformational purpose".

Silvia Salinas Mulder, President,
International Organization for Cooperation in Evaluation; and Chair, Latin American and Caribbean Monitoring, Evaluation and Systematization Network (ReLAC)

"The need for high-quality evaluation to inform decision-making has been emphasized in the 2030 Agenda. But conducting evaluation in contexts of fragility, conflict and violence is very challenging. This book is thus a significantly useful resource and a milestone in this area: it fulfils a long-standing need to provide technical insights on conducting evaluations in contexts of fragility, conflict and violence. The book was prepared and published within the context of the EvalPartners' peer-to-peer project, an experience likely contributing to making its insights richer and deeper. I congratulate the authors and organizations involved in this effort for this important contribution to the global evaluation community".

Marco Segone, Director, Evaluation Office, United Nations Population Fund;
Former Chair, United Nations Evaluation Group; and Founder, EvalPartners

"Both aid and evaluation must be adapted to address fragility and conflict, especially under the current global crisis caused by COVID-19. While fragility and conflict demand decisive and intense attention from aid agencies, the very same circumstances impose great challenges on the delivery of such aid. Strategy, programme and project design are difficult; commitment from recipient parties is fragile; and implementation is uncertain and often subject to strong reversals. By the same token, evaluating the relevance, significance, effectiveness and impact of aid efforts under these circumstances is a complex endeavour. How can one evaluator assess the relevance of aid efforts in an unstable environment? How to rate implementation work in the face of crisis and broken institutional capacities? What about assessing the efficacy, effectiveness and efficiency of the support while recognizing reversals? And how to deal with the challenges of collecting evidence and ensuring minimum utilization of evaluation findings to improve further aid efforts? This publication is a welcome initiative contributing to the stock of knowledge on ways to answer these questions and reminding development practitioners that during conflicts and pandemics and in fragile circumstances in general, monitoring and evaluation matter more than ever. I congratulate the authors, under the leadership of Hur Hassnain, as well as IDEAS and its collaborators for their timely and extremely useful contribution to our discipline".

Marvin Taylor-Dormond, Director General of Independent Evaluation,
Asian Development Bank

"The world order has become increasingly volatile. Inequality has risen to intolerable levels, climate change and environmental degradation bring increasing uncertainty, and pandemics threaten both human health and societal development. The World Bank estimates that by 2030 two-thirds of the extreme poor will live in countries characterized by fragility, conflict and violence. Research has shown that rising temperatures and decreasing precipitation raise the occurrence of conflict. At the same time, pandemics are on the rise as humankind encroaches on the natural environment through the expansion of economic activities, thereby providing opportunities for pathogens to spill over to humans. This new reality requires evaluation in order to remain relevant to rethink its approaches and assume a holistic perspective at the nexus of development and the environment. As evaluators, we must embrace new perspectives and methodologies that allow us to analyse complex situations beyond individual projects and to contribute solutions to complex problems. This book is an important step in enhancing our repertoire for designing and conducting meaningful evaluations in challenging contexts defined by fragility, conflict and violence".

Juha I. Uitto, Director,
Independent Evaluation Office, Global Environment Facility

Contents

Boxes

Figures

Tables

Foreword: EvalPartners Co-Chair

The challenges our planet faces today are immense. They range from the growing impact of changing climate to rising hunger in an age of plenty. It is increasingly clear that environmental degradation is triggering a rise in pandemics that threaten both human health and social and economic development across the globe.

Five years into the era of the Sustainable Development Goals, the evidence is overwhelming that the world is still far off course in achieving the global goals and that instead we are in a period of crisis and conflict.

In the past decade emergency situations have risen dramatically, and conflicts have become more protracted – devastating lives and livelihoods, predominantly in areas where resilience is low and fragility high.

The *2020 Global Report on Food Crises* paints a picture in which 8 out of 10 of the world's major food crises are characterized by situations of conflict and insecurity as key drivers of acute hunger (FSIN 2020). In 2018, the United Nations Security Council adopted Resolution 2417, acknowledging the link between conflict and hunger and condemning the use of starvation as a weapon of war.

For the World Food Programme (WFP), the recent emphasis on the importance of peacebuilding could not have come at a more critical moment. In 2020, the Nobel Peace Prize was awarded to the WFP for its efforts to combat hunger – its contribution to peace in conflict-affected areas.

These are significant markers as the WFP, together with the international community, dedicates greater attention to generating evidence around the complex issues underpinning the humanitarian-development-peace nexus.

For the evaluation community, this reality requires us to innovate our approaches and embrace a holistic and systematic perspective that envelops nexus thinking. It pushes us to consider new perspectives and approaches that allow us to analyse complex situations beyond individual projects and initiatives and to contribute to the identification of durable solutions to wicked problems.

This means we must be ready and equipped to perform in challenging contexts. Conflict and violence present significant challenges for evaluators in many ways: identifying and accessing affected populations, collecting data in unsafe environments, understanding power dynamics, and confronting fear and suspicion. All this together with the need to apply humanitarian principles, adopt a do no harm approach, promote sound ethical practice and protection, and respect conflict-sensitive programming.

In fragile and conflict-affected environments, evaluation evidence is needed more than ever to shine a light on what is working, what is not and what can be done to tackle the deep-seated root causes and inequalities that spark conflict and violence. In order to gather this evidence, we must be ready and equipped to perform in challenging contexts, apply humanitarian principles, promote sound ethical practice and protection, and respect conflict-sensitive programming.

This book is perfectly timed as an essential guide to help evaluators become better equipped, and contribute to evaluation practice that demonstrates its relevance and delivers on its potentially transformative purpose.

Featuring valuable contributions from seasoned experts in our field, this book offers useful advice from the early stages of understanding power and conflict to the final stages of reporting findings, together with practical information about choosing methods and protecting evaluation teams and communities.

Many of the elements included in this book will have an immediate purpose in strengthening the work of my own evaluation function at the WFP. More broadly, it will help the global evaluation community enhance our repertoire for designing and conducting meaningful evaluations in challenging contexts defined by fragility, conflict and violence.

I congratulate the authors and the contributors involved in this valuable contribution to global evaluation practice.

Andrea Cook
Director, Evaluation, World Food Programme
Co-Chair, EvalPartners

Foreword: IDEAS President

This book is coming out at a time when the world is facing an unprecedented global humanitarian crisis. More than 3 million people have died due to the COVID-19 pandemic, and many more deaths are unfortunately expected. The crisis has exacerbated inequalities, levels of poverty and violence throughout the world. The environmental impact is also tremendous. Countries, especially those of the global South, are at serious risk of not progressing towards the Sustainable Development Goals (SDGs). Policy- and decision-makers are being called on to make smart and important decisions to reduce the effects of the current global crisis and to accelerate progress towards the SDGs.

In the current situation, more than ever, the world needs evaluation. There is undeniably a need for evidence to inform effective decision- and policymaking. Evaluation is to be seen not only as an agent but as a hope for lasting and transformative change.

This book aims to contribute to generate a dialogue on why, how and for what purpose to evaluate in contexts of fragility, conflict and violence. It builds upon the knowledge and practical experience of evaluation professionals of various organizations and regions, thus showing a diversity of perspectives and experiences.

IDEAS – the International Development Evaluation Association – is proud to launch this book, which we believe could not be more relevant or timely. This book forms part of a series of initiatives IDEAS is undertaking to advocate for and contribute to transformational evaluation. On behalf of IDEAS, I would like invite and encourage evaluators, policymakers and the wider community to read it and to promote its use.

Ada Ocampo
President
IDEAS

Acknowledgements

This book is an initiative of the IDEAS (International Development Evaluation Association) Thematic Interest Group on Evaluation in Fragility, Conflict and Violence (EvalFCV). It includes contributions from evaluation experts from the Global South and the Global North and from a variety of institutions including international development banks, bilateral and multilateral aid agencies, academia and civil society organizations to promote evaluations in fragility and conflict.

The book was initially developed as guidance to conduct evaluation workshops on the topic in Afghanistan and Pakistan, with financial support from an EvalPartner Peer to Peer grant to the Afghanistan Evaluation Society, the Canadian Evaluation Society and the Pakistan Evaluation Association. Since then, the material has been presented on various platforms including the Organisation for Economic Co-operation and Development/ Development Assistance Committee's EvalNet and the United Nations Evaluation Group Partnership Forum in June 2020, the U.K. Department for International Development's Evaluation Cadre Professional Development Conference in January 2020, and the IDEAS Global Assembly in Prague in October 2019. The authors' own contributions were greatly enriched through robust discussions and group work at various forums and workshops.

Hur Hassnain provided overall leadership and management in writing and developing the book. The book's co-authors were Anupam Anand, Inga-Lill Aronsson, Sarah Davies, Gabrielle Duffy, Lauren Kelly, Wanda Krause, Keiko Kuji-Shikatani, Marco Lorenzoni, Rhiannon McHugh, Emma Rotondo, Wendy Rowe, Simona Somma, Melinda Sutherland and Serge Eric Yakeu.

The individual contributors and reviewers are too numerous to list here, but a few should be mentioned for their particular support: Marie-Hélène Adrien, Michael Bamberger, Anna Chernova, Andrea Cook, François Dupaquier, Marie Gaarder, Michelle Garred, Alena Koscalova, Kathleen Latimer, Samandar Mahmodi, Cristina Magro, Linda Morra Imas, Arjan Schuthof, Marco Segone, Gene Shackman, Marvin Taylor-Dormond and Rob van den Berg.

And finally, thanks to Nita Congress for editing this publication and to Tatsunori Kano for allowing us to use his artwork for the cover page and in the body of the book.

Hur Hassnain
Lead Author
hurhassnain@hotmail.com

Contributors

LEAD AUTHOR

Hur Hassnain (London, United Kingdom), Board Member, International Development Evaluation Association; Founder, Pakistan Evaluation Association (corresponding author: hurhassnain@hotmail.com)

CO-AUTHORS

Anupam Anand (Washington, D.C., USA), Evaluation Officer, Independent Evaluation Office, Global Environment Facility

Inga-Lill Aronsson (Uppsala, Sweden), Senior Lecturer in Museum and Cultural Heritage Studies, Uppsala University

Sarah Davies (Oxford, UK), Evaluation and Communications Specialist, i4D Consulting Ltd; former Global Advisor, Strategic Learning and Communications, Oxfam Great Britain

Gabrielle Duffy (Rome, Italy), Independent Consultant; former Senior Evaluation Officer, World Food Programme

Lauren Kelly (Washington, D.C., USA), Lead Evaluation Officer and Fragility, Conflict and Violence Specialist, Independent Evaluation Group, World Bank Group

Wanda Krause (Victoria, British Columbia, Canada), Associate Professor, School of Leadership; Program Head, Global Leadership Program, Royal Roads University

Keiko Kuji-Shikatani (Ottawa, Canada), Education Officer, Ontario Ministry of Education; Credentialing Board Member, Canadian Evaluation Society

Marco Lorenzoni (Brussels, Belgium), Senior Evaluator; Team Leader of the Evaluation Support Service, a Technical Assistance of the European Commission Directorate-General for International Partnerships

Rhiannon McHugh (London, UK), Evaluation Adviser, UK Foreign Commonwealth and Development Office

Emma Rotondo (Lima, Peru), Independent Consultant; Co-Chair, Latin American and Caribbean Monitoring, Evaluation and Systematization Network (ReLAC) Evalrights; Member, Board of Directors, EvalPeru

Wendy Rowe (Victoria, British Columbia, Canada), Professor, School of Leadership, Royal Roads University

Simona Somma (Rome, Italy), Evaluation Specialist, Independent Office of Evaluation, International Fund for Agricultural Development

Melinda Sutherland (Manila, the Philippines), Senior Evaluation Specialist, Asian Development Bank

Serge Eric Yakeu (Yaoundé, Cameroon), Evaluation Expert and Visiting Professor; Global Chair of EvalIndigenous; Vice-President, IDEAS

Abbreviations

ALNAP	Active Learning Network for Accountability and Performance
DAC	Development Assistance Committee
EvalFCV	Evaluation in Fragility, Conflict, and Violence
FCDO	Foreign, Commonwealth and Development Office (formerly Department for International Development – DFID)
FCV	fragility, conflict and violence
GPS	Global Positioning System
ICT	information and communication technology
IDEAS	International Development Evaluation Association
MDG	Millennium Development Goal
NASA	National Aeronautics and Space Administration
OECD	Organisation for Economic Co-operation and Development
PNG	Papua New Guinea
SDG	Sustainable Development Goal
SMS	short message service
VIIRS	Visible Infrared Imaging Radiometer Suite
WFP	World Food Programme

Introduction

This book is a guide to designing, managing and conducting evaluations in fragile and conflict-affected countries and/or contexts that are affected by fragility, conflict and violence (FCV). Such countries or contexts may present challenges for evaluation that, if not properly addressed or mitigated, can adversely affect the validity and results of the evaluation. Mitigating these challenges can entail significant effort, and can sometimes require redefining the direction, purpose or scope of the evaluation.

Fragile and conflict-affected contexts are characterized by "weak state policies and institutions, undermining the countries' capacity to deliver services to their citizens, control corruption, or provide for sufficient voice and accountability; and are at risk of conflict and political instability" (Brown and Langer 2012). The World Bank's list of fragile and conflict-affected situations for fiscal years 2006–20 is available at http://pubdocs.worldbank.org/en/176001594407411053/FCSList-FY06toFY20.pdf.

Additionally, evaluation – like development aid itself – can unintentionally exacerbate tensions in ways that negatively affect conflict-affected populations if care is not taken to develop and integrate conflict sensitivity into the evaluation's design and approaches. There is an evolving body of literature on conflict sensitivity in the design and monitoring of development, humanitarian and conflict prevention assistance (e.g. Goldwyn and Chigas 2013; United Nations and World Bank 2018), but literature on how to design and conduct evaluations in FCV contexts is scarce.

CONTEXT

Two billion people live in countries where development outcomes are affected by FCV (Hoogeveen and Pape 2020). The World Bank estimates that by 2030, up to two-thirds of the global extreme poor will be living in fragile and conflict-affected situations, making it evident that without intensified action, global poverty goals will not be met (Corral et al. 2020). Further, the Organisation for Economic Co-operation and Development (OECD) considers that without action the percentage living in FCV situations will exceed 80 per cent (OECD 2018).

Global attention and development aid are increasingly focused on supporting prevention and early response interventions to address drivers of conflict. For example, the International Development Association (IDA), the arm of the World Bank Group that helps the world's poorest countries, has committed to doubling its financing for fragile states. Concurrently, restrictions and security concerns around deploying staff in fragile countries have pushed national and international aid agencies to rely on various new and innovative methods such as remote sensing, information and communication technologies (ICTs), and third-party monitoring techniques to collect data and report on intervention results.

Moving beyond FCV contexts, as evaluation data collection methods continue to evolve, there is a need for a more comprehensive repository that assembles guidance from different sources to facilitate learning about different approaches to conducting evaluation in conflict-, climate- and gender-sensitive ways. Challenges hindering evaluation efforts in FCV contexts include, but are not limited to, the following:

- Difficulties in identifying and accessing the affected populations
- Understanding power and relationship dynamics
- Fear and sensitivity around fact-finding missions and perceived grievances
- Limited availability of good-quality data
- Methodological requirements, with particular attention to unintended effects
- Lack of appropriate tools and resources
- Indications of corruption and human rights violations that are difficult to validate and report on.

Other challenges may include **identifying competent evaluators** who are willing to travel to conflict-affected areas, and **impartiality** throughout the evaluation process given the political contexts and difficulty in engaging with all key players. Environments that are experiencing FCV also tend to be politically volatile; and it can be difficult to identify and engage with the key stakeholders to have them on board for a robust evaluation process. It can be challenging to find the appropriate direction, purpose and scope for the evaluation – sometimes this has to be redefined when in the field.

The *SDG16 Progress Report* by the Institute for Economics and Peace highlights that fragile and conflict-affected countries were on average 25 per cent more likely to have missed their Millennium Development Goals (MDGs) than other countries, as shown in figure 1. Figure 1 also shows that only 16 per cent of fragile and conflict-affected countries met the targets or made progress on them. The remainder were either off target or had no data at all. The report notes that

> MDG indicators for which the majority of fragile and conflict-affected countries recorded the poorest results were those that addressed child mortality, maternal health and environmental sustainability. No conflict-affected country achieved the goal of reducing by two-thirds the under-five mortality rate between 1990 and 2015. Additionally, many of the fragile and conflict-affected countries have difficulty in maintaining the necessary systems to adequately capture the data. This can lead to poor quality data, resulting in situations appearing worse or better than what they are. (IEP 2017, 7)

Figure 1 **Average progress in MDGs by country classification**

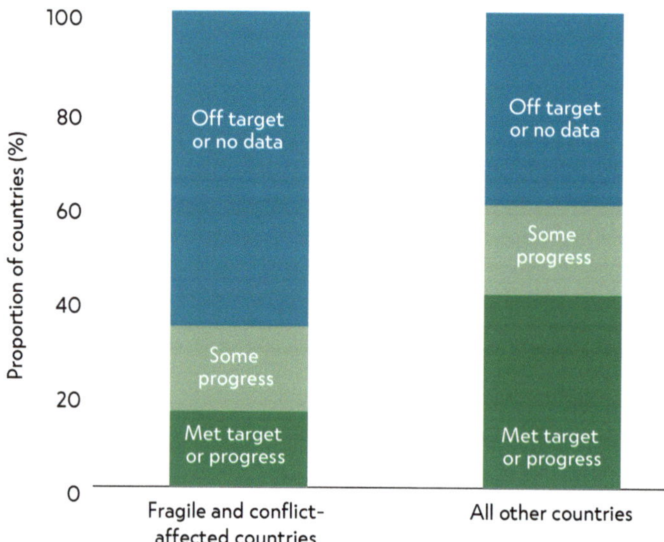

Source: IEP 2017, based on World Bank and IEP calculations.

This lack of data could be attributed to a lack of investment in and/or knowledge of how to do monitoring and evaluation in contexts that are fluid, complex and sometimes volatile (IEP 2017).

The OECD, in its *States of Fragility 2018* report highlights that fragile states are at the most risk of not achieving the Sustainable Development Goals (OECD 2018). The Overseas Development Institute reports,

> Many vulnerable refugees and internally displaced people (IDPs) are hosted in fragile and conflict affected states. And there are most likely many more that the data doesn't capture. With the number of violent conflicts doubling since 2000 and displacement on an upward trend, these populations could continue to grow. However, there is limited accountability for meeting these populations' needs and ensuring that they are not left behind. (Samman et al. 2018, 8)

Existing socioeconomic challenges faced by lower- and middle-income countries have been exacerbated by the global COVID-19 pandemic, leading to an increased likelihood of violence and political instability. In its recent report on COVID-19, the Institute for Economics and Peace notes, "Most indicators in the Global Peace Index are expected to deteriorate. The one area that may improve is military expenditure, as countries redirect resources to propping up their economies" (IEP 2020, 2).

With so many people living in vulnerable situations, it is of paramount importance that the right conditions are created to ensure rigorous and sensitive data collection and evaluation in FCV contexts.

ORGANIZATION

This book is organized in three phases and seven steps, in accordance with typical evaluation practice.

Phase A: Designing the evaluation

- Step 1: Understand and adapt to the context
- Step 2: Select evaluation methods and tools
- Step 3: Select the evaluation team

Phase B: Conducting the evaluation

- Step 4: Organize field mission for data collection
- Step 5: Arrange for remote data collection
- Step 6: Close the evaluation learning loop

Phase C: Using the evaluation

- Step 7: Report, disseminate and use

In addition to boxes, tables and figures providing specific examples, data and illustrations, the main text is supplemented by tips, notes and techniques (in blue) and further reading (in green). The book also includes an appendix that defines key concepts referenced in the main text.

Figure 2 presents the approach and structure of this book by phase and step. The seven steps are not necessarily sequential, and some can be taken iteratively – for example, step 3 could be done before Step 2 or Dissemination work in the Step 7 could start during the data collection stage.

Figure 2 **Seven steps for evaluation in FCV contexts**

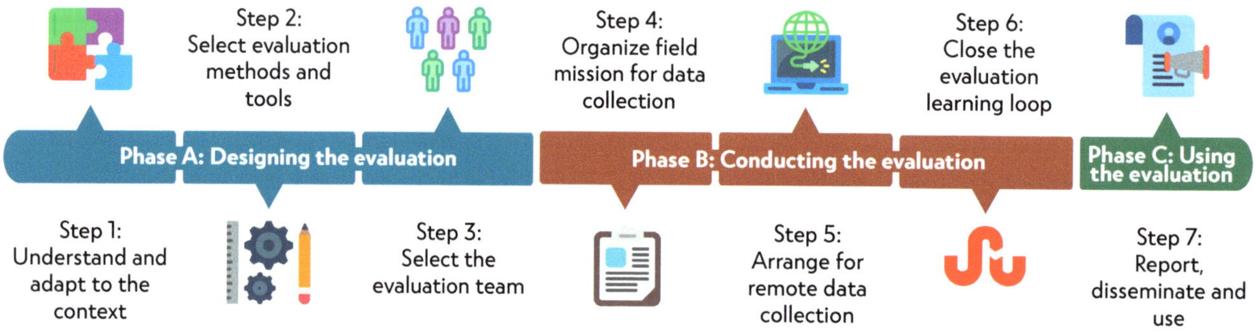

Phase A: Designing the evaluation
Step 1: Understand and adapt to the context
Step 2: Select evaluation methods and tools
Step 3: Select the evaluation team

Phase B: Conducting the evaluation
Step 4: Organize field mission for data collection
Step 5: Arrange for remote data collection
Step 6: Close the evaluation learning loop

Phase C: Using the evaluation
Step 7: Report, disseminate and use

HOW TO USE THIS BOOK

The IDEAS' EvalFCV Thematic Interest Group is a network that serves as a catalyst to promote evaluations in contexts of fragility, conflict and violence. Follow on Twitter at @EvalFCV; join by writing to Hur Hassnain at hurhassnain@hotmail.com.

This book is aimed at everyone who might be engaged in an evaluation in an FCV context, including commissioners and evaluators. Conducting an evaluation in an FCV context entails operating in a situation that is unpredictable and constantly changing. Flexibility is therefore essential. All the steps presented in this book are critical; some may be more relevant or of greater or lesser importance given the particular situation and audience.

We suggest using this book alongside other resources and toolkits referenced here and/or available otherwise. Further, the techniques for evaluation given in this book should be employed to complement and supplement those applied in stable contexts. As explained by the U.K. Department for International Development (now the Foreign, Commonwealth and Development Office): "Techniques for measuring and managing results in fragile and conflict-affected situations are not fundamentally different to those we use in peaceful and stable countries, but may need to be employed more intensively, and adapted and combined with innovative approaches" (DFID n.d., 3).

A final note: Throughout, we use the term "intervention" to refer generically to projects, programmes, policy dialogues, etc.

PHASE A

Designing the Evaluation

The War Child night ambulance provides medical attention to street children and, where feasible, gathers data to improve intervention quality and support, Tshangu, Democratic Republic of Congo. Photo: Zute Lightfoot

Step 1: **Understand and Adapt to the Context**

Interventions implemented in contexts of fragility, conflict and violence (FCV) often operate in a politically complex environment and deal with complicated issues that may be difficult to measure and report on. The first step for evaluators in such circumstances is to develop a comprehensive and holistic understanding of the context in which they work – including its key cultural, social, economic and political factors; the proximate and structural drivers of conflict and their interplay; and key actors.

This emphasis on understanding and adapting to contextual factors is not unique to FCV contexts, but in fact applies to the evaluation of any intervention. In FCV contexts, however, the need to understand the cultural, socioeconomic and political context as well as drivers of conflict and key actors is critical given the inherent complexities of such contexts. An example highlighted at the 2019 Pakistan Evaluation Conference and EvalFCV Workshop in Islamabad involved an evaluation exercise on the use of contraceptives by young people in Pakistan. Because the enumerators lacked an understanding of the social and cultural context, they faced problems speaking to and obtaining data from young married women and girls; this affected the validity of the data and the evaluation. Box 1.1 presents another example from Papua New Guinea.

Programmes in FCV contexts operate in a sensitive political environment and address complex challenges that are often hard to measure and report on. To evaluate them, the first task for evaluators is to build a comprehensive, systemic understanding of the context in which they are to work, including underlying cultural, social, economic and political factors and their interplay (Aronsson and Hassnain 2019).

To ensure full understanding of the evaluation context, Step 1 comprises the following:

- Conduct conflict analysis in line with the evaluation scope and intervention context
- Conduct gender analysis
- Conduct safeguarding and protection analysis
- Conduct stakeholder analysis
- Conduct evaluability assessment

Box 1.1 **The critical importance of understanding and adapting to context: Papua New Guinea**

Papua New Guinea (PNG) has approximately 850 unique language groups spread across 8 million people residing in rugged mountainous terrain and an extensive archipelago. The cultural diversity, coupled with high levels of poverty, low levels of human development, and weak governance and capacity, make PNG a highly complex development environment. Markers of fragility in PNG include (i) weak governance and institutional capacity combined with corruption, all of which impair growth and poverty alleviation efforts; (ii) inadequate security and service delivery functions, resulting in a highly volatile legal and judicial context; and (iii) high vulnerability to natural disasters and climate change. PNG is located around the tropical region and along the Pacific Ring of Fire, and is prone to natural disasters including earthquakes, volcanic eruptions, floods, cyclones, landslides, tsunamis and king tides.

In February 2018 a 7.5 magnitude earthquake devastated the Hela and Southern Highlands Provinces and significantly affected the Western and Enga Provinces. The earthquake claimed the lives of 160 people, displaced 11,671 households (58,300 people) and caused a significant economic loss for the country. The earthquake exacerbated the fragile operating environment in a province that was already highly volatile and prone to tribal and clan fighting. Understanding and adapting to heightened FCV (which continued in the aftermath of the earthquake) was integral to development partners providing rapid emergency assistance and longer-term recovery support. This was similarly crucial for evaluation teams subsequently analysing whether the aid ultimately provided the vital assistance as intended and in the places of greatest impact.

Source: Case study report by Melinda Sutherland.

CONDUCT CONFLICT ANALYSIS

In contexts that are or have been fluid, complex and insecure, understanding the conflict itself is a critical starting point. The evaluation should seek to integrate sensitive and timely conflict analysis throughout the process into its design, approach, reporting and dissemination.

Context analysis versus conflict analysis: Context analysis considers the social, economic, political and cultural issues; conflict analysis focuses specifically on the conflict – how it started, what it entails, who it affects, etc.

Purpose

A conflict analysis allows evaluators to:

- Understand the background, history and causes of the conflict – all of which affect development decision-making and the outcomes of the intervention under assessment
- Identify all the relevant groups involved
- Understand the perspectives of these groups and how they relate to each other
- Identify and understand the drivers of conflict
- Understand how the evaluation could interact with the conflict and the conflict drivers, and thus have the potential to exacerbate conflict drivers and so escalate conflicts – or conversely reduce future conflict and its risks

Methods

An in-depth conflict analysis can be time-consuming and expensive, as it requires the collection of data that are not readily available and a widely triangulated process at multiple levels (national and local). While for some interventions, a conflict analysis may have been conducted to inform intervention design, this would need to be updated by the time the evaluation takes place.

An evaluator may want to consider more readily available open sources of analysis and data to begin the conflict analysis process. The International Crisis Group, among other organizations, regularly updates its conflict analysis data. Specific conflict data can be obtained from the Armed Conflict Location and Event Data (ACLED) project and Uppsala Conflict Data Program (UCDP), although these data are not without their limitations. Additionally, some aid agencies have developed conflict assessment tools that can be accessed and adapted, such as the German Federal Ministry for Economic Cooperation and Development's Peace and Conflict Assessment methodological framework (BMZ, GIZ and KfW 2014).

Where possible, national and international counterparts should be consulted to inform the conflict analysis. This activity may require hiring a specialized consultant and can entail risk, especially for nationals of FCV countries. Hence, any interview and interaction with stakeholders should take place in discreet locations and the data should be anonymous.

Piggybacking on the data and findings of conflict analysis conducted by other organizations is very useful in avoiding overlapping efforts in data collection and wasting resources. Such external analysis should ideally be verified with the appropriate stakeholders; realistically, however, in FCV situations, organizations may not readily share such material. Given the sensitivity of the information involved, preparing and signing specific protocols to protect confidentiality may facilitate the disclosure of such analyses to the evaluation team.

The conflict analysis should revolve around the following questions:

- What are the sources of tension and cohesion in the communities?
- What are the key proximate and structural causes and drivers of conflict and violence?
- What are the conflict dynamics?
- What are the likely future conflict scenarios/triggers?
- Who are the key conflict actors? What power dynamics are in play? What actions are required to overcome socioeconomic, political and security challenges?
- What are the sources of resilience?
- Are there opportunities for increasing peace and stability?
- Where and how might aid unintentionally exacerbate inter- or intra-group conflict?

For conflict analysis resources, see:

UK Government Stabilisation Unit (2019), "Monitoring Evaluation and Learning (MEL) in Conflict and Stabilisation Settings – A Guidance Note": https://www.gov.uk/government/publications/monitoring-evaluation-and-learning-mel-in-conflict-and-stabilisation-settings-a-guidance-note

UK Government Stabilisation Unit (2016), "Conflict Sensitivity: Tools and Guidance": https://www.gov.uk/government/publications/conflict-sensitivity-tools-and-guidance

H. Haider (2014), "Conflict Sensitivity: Topic Guide": https://gsdrc.org/topic-guides/conflict-sensitivity/

Conflict Sensitivity Consortium (2012), "How to Guide to Conflict Sensitivity", chapter 2: https://gsdrc.org/document-library/how-to-guide-to-conflict-sensitivity/

BMZ, GIZ and KfW (2014), "Peace and Conflict Assessment Guidance".

Box 1.2 **Gender analysis in Papua New Guinea**

After the 2018 earthquake in Papua New Guinea (PNG), gender analysis was undertaken as part of the humanitarian emergency response and recovery and subsequent evaluations and evaluation missions. PNG ranks very low on all global indicators in advancing gender equality and eliminating violence against women; these tendencies are particularly evident among the patriarchal tribes of the affected Highlands provinces. Rapid analysis after the earthquake verified that the key issues facing women in the region were the high level of violence against women and girls; the need for greater economic empowerment, including access to safe markets; and the low level of women's involvement in national decision-making. It is estimated that over 66 per cent of all PNG women will suffer some form of physical or sexual violence in their lifetime, 41 per cent of PNG men have admitted to having raped someone, and 7.7 per cent of men admit to having perpetrated male rape. These data pointed to the need to provide support to conflict-affected areas in locations that were known to be the safest for both women and men, such as through churches as opposed to community halls. Gender analysis of conflict was also integral to ensuring the safety of the men and women providing emergency assistance and, subsequently, evaluating the support that was provided. For example, community consultations were undertaken with women in rurally based churches.

CONDUCT GENDER ANALYSIS

For tips on how to measure women's and girls' empowerment, see J-PAL (2018), "A Practical Guide to Measuring Women's and Girls' Empowerment in Impact Evaluations": https://www.povertyactionlab.org/practical-guide-measuring-womens-and-girls-empowerment-impact-evaluations

Understanding the gender dynamics within a particular context is a crucial step that should be included in every evaluation design (box 1.2). Studies show that gender inequalities can contribute to conflict via intersections with other conflict drivers – e.g. existing ethno-national and economic power relations (Cockburn 2010). Field experience and research show that women and men, and boys and girls, experience, engage in and are affected by violent conflict in different ways. In many cases, conflict increases the burden on women. Systemic violation of women's rights and their exclusion from economic, social and political spheres are barriers to development and may affect conflict dynamics (OECD 2012).

Purpose

A gender/gender-sensitive conflict analysis identifies the different needs and priorities of women, men, girls, boys and sexual and gender minorities. It seeks to understand the extent to which existing gender norms and behaviours interact with conflict dynamics. For example, gender disparities could be attributed to unequal power dynamics within social, economic and political systems and structures. A gender conflict analysis can bring visibility to any violence used to maintain power in public and private spaces and sheds light on any overlaps that may exist between these two spaces. It should also look at the availability, quality and degree of implementation of gender mainstreaming strategies in the design of the intervention.

For a combined look at conflict sensitivity and gender, see CDA Collaborative Learning Projects 2018 publication, "Do No Harm and Gender: A Guidance Note": https://www.cdacollaborative.org/publication/no-harm-gender-guidance-note/

Without a gender conflict analysis to inform the evaluation planning, there is a risk of exacerbating the inequalities, injustice, discrimination and disempowerment that may have fuelled instability and violence.

Methods

Development interventions in all contexts should have a plan for how to address gender-related issues and ensure gender sensitivity. Such plans are critical in FCV contexts, given the prevalence of gender-based violence, and the correlation between gender inequality and certain types of conflict. The role of the evaluation is to assess the quality of the gender analysis conducted and how gender-sensitive the intervention was in the specific context. The conflict and gender analysis need only to be looked at in relation to the intervention being evaluated. For example, for an evaluation of an intervention in Iraq, a gender and conflict analysis is needed for that intervention only, not necessarily for the whole of Iraq.

If a gender analysis has not been previously conducted, evaluators should try to use existing gender assessments – conducted by the same organization or other entities – or any other available resources that can complement the conflict analysis and fill this gap by providing useful insights for the evaluation design.

A gender-sensitive conflict analysis can be carried out at different levels (regional, national, local) according to its purpose. For a specific intervention or evaluation, a local-level analysis is more likely to be required.

Key questions in conducting a gender analysis include the following:

- What are the different needs, aspirations and risks of women and men, boys and girls, and sexual and gender minorities in the conflict situation?
- How are gender roles affected by the conflict? How do experiences of the conflict vary for different men, women and gender minorities according to different aspects of their identity (intersectionality)?
- What roles are being played and by whom in bringing about a peaceful resolution to the conflict?

For further gender analysis resources, see:

Saferworld, WILPF and Oxfam (2017), "Building Inclusive Peace: Gender at the Heart of Conflict Analysis". https://wilpf.org/wp-content/uploads/2018/01/BuildingInclusivePeace-GenderHeartConflictAnalysis.pdf

Saferworld (2016), "Gender Analysis of Conflict Toolkit". https://www.saferworld.org.uk/resources/publications/1076-gender-analysis-of-conflict

Conciliation Resources (2015), "Gender and Conflict Analysis Toolkit for Peacebuilders". https://www.c-r.org/resource/gender-and-conflict-analysis-toolkit-peacebuilders

Saferworld (2020), "Gender-Sensitive Conflict Analysis Workshop Facilitation Guide". https://www.saferworld.org.uk/resources/publications/1284-gender-sensitive-conflict-analysis-a-facilitation-guide

UN Women (2013): "How to Manage Gender-Responsive Evaluation": https://www.unwomen.org/en/digital-library/publications/2015/4/un-women-evaluation-handbook-how-to-manage-gender-responsive-evaluation

European Institute for Gender Equality website, https://eige.europa.eu/

United Nations Evaluation Group (2014), "Guidance on Integrating Human Rights and Gender Equality in Evaluations": http://www.unevaluation.org/document/detail/1616

European Commission (2018), "Evaluation with Gender as a Cross-Cutting Dimension".

Bridge/UNDP (2007), "Gender and Indicators Overview Report": http://content-ext.undp.org/aplaws_publications/1850960/GenderandIndicators.pdf

CONDUCT SAFEGUARDING AND PROTECTION ANALYSIS

Safeguarding is the responsibility of organizations to make sure their staff, operations and interventions do no harm to at-risk children and adults or expose them to abuse or exploitation. It is good practice to think about how to safeguard everyone in organizations at all times, including protecting staff from harm and inappropriate behaviour such as bullying and harassment.

Many organizations have chosen to develop standard safeguarding principles that can be used as a benchmark of minimum standards for staff and partners. For example, the safeguarding principles that underpin the due diligence of the U.K.'s Foreign, Commonwealth and Development Office (FCDO; formerly the Department for International Development – DFID) are summarized in box 1.3. This can help foster a

Box 1.3 FCDO principles of safeguarding

- Everyone has responsibility for safeguarding.
- Do no harm.
- Organizations have a safeguarding duty of care to beneficiaries, staff and volunteers, including where downstream partners are part of delivery. This includes children and vulnerable adults in the community who are not direct beneficiaries but may be vulnerable to abuse.
- Act with integrity, be transparent and accountable.
- All activity is done in the best interest of the child/vulnerable person.
- A child is defined as someone under the age of 18 regardless of the age of majority/consent in country.
- All children shall be treated equally, irrespective of race, gender, religion/or none, sexual orientation or disability.
- Organizations that work with children and vulnerable adults should apply a safeguarding lens to their promotional communications and fundraising activities.

These principles align with the United Nations Convention on the Rights of the Child (UNCRC).

Source: FCDO 2020.

safeguarding environment and an organizational culture that protects people from unintended harm.

Protection analysis helps to analyse risks and avoid potential negative consequences to specific population groups in situations of conflict, instability and pandemic. The World Food Programme suggests that to ensure interventions are safe, dignified and mindful of people's varied circumstances, needs, rights and capacities, protection considerations must be incorporated throughout the intervention cycle. Protection analyses are most effective when carried out prior to intervention design or during monitoring and evaluation. They can, however, be undertaken at any stage of the intervention cycle to inform intervention implementation (WFP 2016).

It is good practice for the evaluation team to be aware of an organization's commitments to safeguarding and protection and to understand the protocols to follow if concerns arise. Where possible, evaluators should conduct a safeguarding analysis to ensure evaluation safeguards protect those at risk. If the organization does not have a commitment to safeguarding or has not carried out protection analysis, the evaluators can do so as a stand-alone exercise or in conjunction with other assessments such as the conflict analysis or gender analysis. The latter modality is preferable, as it avoids exposing the same affected group/individuals to several separate assessments.

For more on safeguarding and protection, see:

World Food Programme, Protection Guidance Manual: https://docs.wfp.org/api/documents/WFP-0000013164/download/

BOND, Safeguarding Toolkit: https://www.bond.org.uk/resources/safeguarding-toolkit

FCDO (2020), "Enhanced Due Diligence: Safeguarding for External Partners": https://www.gov.uk/guidance/safeguarding-against-sexual-exploitation-and-abuse-and-sexual-harassment-seah-in-the-aid-sector

The protection analysis should seek to answer the following key questions (WFP 2016):

- To what safeguarding/protection risks are women, men, girls and boys exposed? Do people pursue negative coping mechanisms, such as child labour, transactional sex, and irregular migration or smuggling? Are they vulnerable to hazardous or exploitative working arrangements or human trafficking? Is people's safety threatened by conflict or violent crime? Are some people marginalized or not able to access basic services?
- Who is affected and how? Men, women, boys, girls, sexual and gender minorities, different age groups, ethnic groups, and people with special needs all may be affected differently.
- What/who is the cause of risks and what are their motivations?
- Are safeguarding/protection risks created by the intervention? Are people at risk when they access assistance or participate in the intervention? Which people? Does the intervention inadvertently create or exacerbate household or community tensions? For whom? How?

CONDUCT STAKEHOLDER ANALYSIS

Identifying stakeholders

Michael Quinn Patton, in his book *Utilization Focused Evaluation*, defines evaluation stakeholders as individuals who have a vested interest in the evaluation findings and categorizes these stakeholders into six different groups (Patton 2008):

- Individuals with authority to make intervention decisions (policymakers, funders, advisory boards, etc.)
- Individuals with direct responsibility for the intervention (developers, administration, managers, etc.)
- Intended beneficiaries of the intervention (individuals, families, communities, etc.)
- Individuals who have been disadvantaged by the intervention (those who lost funding opportunities or have otherwise been negatively affected)
- Individuals with indirect interest in the intervention (journalists, taxpayers, etc.)
- Conflicting or corrupting parties or parties using violence as a means – these are not traditional stakeholders per se, but do have a stake in the FCV context that affects the evaluation as well as the intervention

Since most interventions in FCV contexts operate in a political environment under conditions of considerable tension with a full spectrum of people from the powerful to the powerless, an evaluation should consider the views and interests of all stakeholders. These include but are not limited to international aid agencies, civil society organizations, the private sector, national and local government officials, opposition leaders and groups, local community groups, state or non-state armed actors, and beneficiaries. Each of these groups will have their own perspectives on the underlying conditions/issues in the FCV context and how interventions should be designed and implemented. Consequently, each stakeholder group will have different and potentially conflicting perspectives on the purpose and goals of an evaluation. Invest time in a preliminary background analysis to determine who the stakeholders are and how they are affecting or are affected by the intervention/evaluation exercise.

When designing and conducting evaluations, it is important to consider that stakeholder engagement may differ for each type of stakeholder. A careful and thorough mapping exercise can help minimize "evaluation fatigue" among stakeholders and beneficiaries who may have already participated in workshop/interview/survey activities.

A stakeholder mapping is particularly advised in FCV contexts. This involves creating a grid or schematic that maps the power, interest and influence of each stakeholder over the intervention being evaluated.

Engaging with stakeholders

A truly participatory evaluation that engages all stakeholders of an intervention or policy in the evaluation process can be an excellent method to draw in stakeholders and secure their valuable support in the evaluation process and development of relevant and fit-for-purpose evaluation products. In addition, participatory evaluation can improve data collection, reduce the risk of bias and provide opportunities for ongoing learning while also enabling the timely use of evidence to inform critical decision-making in the FCV contexts.

Engage stakeholders in action learning and evaluative enquiry processes. Engaging stakeholders in evaluation processes can be challenging. Rowe (2017) presents a methodology of engagement that creates conditions for learning through action – often referred to as action learning. Through these processes, there is an opportunity to build commitment among stakeholders to support evaluation activities, accurately establish a good direction for the evaluation and learn from the evaluation endeavour to improve or adapt programmatic efforts. There are three broad stages in the Action Learning and Evaluation (ALEval) framework: preparation and development; strategic planning; and intervention implementation, monitoring and evaluation.

There are often practical challenges as to how much time stakeholders can truly invest in evaluation activities when working in difficult contexts. Also, evaluation findings in FCV settings are often needed quickly to inform the forward direction of crisis response, thus limiting the length of the evaluation process. These factors should be taken into consideration when planning how best to approach stakeholder engagement.

Throughout all phases of the evaluation, efforts are made to engage stakeholders in continuous enquiry, dialogue and engagement. The evaluation uses this stakeholder feedback and reflections to make decisions while concurrently carrying out formal monitoring and measurement of intervention activities, outputs, outcomes and impact on beneficiaries and communities.

Form a stakeholder advisory committee. A stakeholder advisory committee is a group of people interested in the outcomes of the evaluation or the intervention; they can provide valuable insights and inputs to the evaluation. Consider establishing a stakeholder advisory committee to:

- Gain additional insight on the context and intervention
- Determine whether there is stakeholder support to carry out an evaluation
- Develop an agreed-upon statement of evaluation purpose and direction
- Create buy-in and support for the evaluation process and final evaluation products

The following guidance can be useful in forming a stakeholder advisory committee:

- Scope out who should be in the committee by prioritizing those stakeholders who will benefit the most or who have the maximum influence on the intervention or evaluation. This should include beneficiaries. Ensure that all key sides in or perspectives on the conflict are represented on the committee if possible. This may entail getting in touch with state or non-state armed groups or de facto governments; this needs to be done carefully and ethically, and in close consultation with the commissioning agency.
- Keep the number of members manageable to ensure the committee can operate efficiently and enable meaningful discussion. Normally, 8–12 members is considered reasonable, but this will depend on the specific context.

- Give sufficient time and attention to facilitating any processes that require inputs from multiple members of the committee, bearing in mind any power and/or conflict dynamics within the committee.
- Ensure all members of the committee understand their role from the outset – i.e. to give advice and contribute to committee conclusions.
- Hold meetings regularly. Make sure there is a plan to guide these meetings and that everyone is aware of it.
- Develop a time line and workplan for the committee.

For more on stakeholder analysis, see World Bank Group (2001), "Tools and Resources on Stakeholder Analysis": http://www1.worldbank.org/publicsector/anticorrupt/PoliticalEconomy/stakeholderreading.htm

The Better Evaluation webpage on participatory approaches discusses different ways to engage stakeholders and provides links to other practical resources: https://www.betterevaluation.org/en/plan/approach/participatory_evaluation

CONDUCT EVALUABILITY ASSESSMENT

International partnerships and development approaches are not one-size-fits-all, but unpredictable, complex and context specific. Adaptations during the life of an intervention, policy design and implementation in response to the demands of the shifting context as well as their priorities are natural to achieve effective results. Before starting an evaluation, investigate if what is being evaluated is evaluable and if the exercise may enhance the organisation's ability to report on the results it achieved. The European Bank for Reconstruction and Development reports that evaluability assessments are relatively cheap and easy to administer, and their pay-offs are large (EBRD 2012).

During an early preparation stage – such as when the evaluation terms of reference are being developed – it is pertinent to conduct an in-depth desk study to understand what to evaluate, why and for whom. This detailed evaluability assessment will highlight whether the evaluation is feasible and appropriate in the given context. Evaluability assessments help determine "the extent to which an activity or project can be evaluated in a reliable and credible fashion" (OECD DAC 2010, 21). They thus inform stakeholders as to the potential feasibility, scope, approach and value for the money of an evaluation.

Fore more on evaluability assessment, see:

R. Davies (2013), "Planning Evaluability Assessments: A Synthesis of the Literature with Recommendations": https://assets.publishing.service.gov.uk/media/57a08a0d40f0b652dd000534/61141-DFIDWorkingPaper40-finalOct13.pdf

M. Trevisan, *Evaluability Assessment: Improving Evaluation Quality and Use*: https://methods.sagepub.com/book/evaluability-assessment

Davies (2013), in a report of a study commissioned by FCDO, states that an evaluability assessment should address three broad types of issues: program design, availability of information and institutional context. The relative emphasis placed on each area is subject to the assessment's timing, with design being the main focus at a quality assessment stage, and information availability and conduciveness relatively more important during implementation and immediately prior to an evaluation.

Evaluability assessments are also useful in clarifying data gaps, along with other relevant evaluation operational issues. This clarification is critical, as data collection and management in FCV contexts are often poorly coordinated. In general, taking time early in the preparation phase to research the data situation should help prevent surprises like missing data at a later stage, which can derail or delay the evaluation process (OECD 2012).

An evaluator accompanying a group of aid workers for an evaluation in Afghanistan.
Photo: François Dupaquier

Step 2: Select Evaluation Methods and Tools

RECONSTRUCT THEORY OF CHANGE

Rigorous evaluations, including those conducted in fragile contexts, reconstruct the intervention's theory of change at the outset of the evaluation process. Ex post reconstruction of the theory of change allows the evaluation to assess not only if but also how and why the intervention has, or has not, had an impact. The theory of change illustrates the causal links, hypotheses and assumptions for achievement of the intervention's intended results; it should be reconstructed, if possible, together with all relevant stakeholders. This effort will also help in understanding the drivers of conflict during the life of the intervention, how and if the intervention had different impacts on specific identity groups, and how to connect the outcomes and indicators with gender and conflict analysis underpinning the evaluation design.

Interventions in FCV contexts often focus on principles that guide innovation that is needed in "improvising rapid responses in crisis conditions" in "complex dynamic environments" (Patton 2018).

Evaluators need to understand both the theory of change and the operating context – while recognizing that there may be competing theories and that the context may be fluid – in order to define clear evaluation questions and, from there, select an appropriate design and tailor methods and tools.

The theory of change seeks to respond to the following questions:

- **What prompted the intervention?** The answer to this question often lies in shared communal values, springing from the realization that something really needs to change and providing the impetus to make the effort to change. For example, the answer might be "Children and youth need to be reunited with their families as soon as possible so their lives can be re-established to support their well-being and development". Interventions aimed at achieving Sustainable Development Goals are similarly value-based, as these are global goals that exemplify shared common values.
- **What were the intervention's intended outcomes?** In a dynamic, constantly changing and unstable context, defining change could be difficult. A common challenge for interventions in FCV contexts is understanding the nature of change an intervention can realistically hope to bring about. To respond to this challenge,

For a step-by-step guide of the theory of change process, see UK Government Stabilisation Unit (2019), "Guidance on MEL in Conflict and Stabilisation Settings", p. 41: https://assets.publishing.service.gov.uk/government/uploads/system/uploads/attachment_data/file/858813/Monitoring__Evaluation_and_Learning__MEL__in_Conflict_and_Stabilisation_Settings_A_Guidance_Note_7_Nov_2019_-_Final_-__1_.pdf the causal pathway – and corresponding results – must be realistic. To help define realistic results, it is useful to think in terms of the level of control that is possible through an intervention. Ensuring that results are clearly defined at the appropriate levels is critical for achieving them (Stabilisation Unit 2019).

- **What did the intervention achieve?** Describe the activities/strategies/tasks/work/effort needed to realize the desired intervention outcome/changes.
- **What were its unintended effects?** The reconstruction of the theory of change is fundamental to identifying the unintended effects of an intervention. Focusing only on expected results can easily lead to overlooking the unexpected or unintended effects, both positive and negative. Unintended negative effects are of particular concern in complex, fluid, unpredictable and volatile contexts such as FCV situations – and can sometimes be quite serious, putting lives at risk by exacerbating or prolonging violence (Zürcher 2017). In a large-scale example, the aid delivery system in 1980s Rwanda was systematically skewed towards exclusion along regional, sectoral and ethnic lines in ways that allegedly contributed towards the 1994 genocide (Uvin 1998).

Two brief examples describing the unintended consequences of an intervention can be found on the Better Evaluation webpage: https://www.betterevaluation.org/en/resources/example/unintended_consequences

UNDERSTAND THE EVALUATION CRITERIA

Evaluation criteria specify the values that will be used in an evaluation of interventions (Peersman 2014). These criteria are at the core of the evaluation methodology and should be in line with the principles and practices set out by the Organisation for Economic Co-operation and Development's Development Assistance Committee (OECD DAC) in its Glossary of Key Terms in Evaluation and Results-Based Management (OECD DAC 2010), the United Nations Evaluation Group in Norms and Standards for Evaluation (UNEG 2017) and Active Learning Network for Accountability and Performance (ALNAP) in Evaluation of Protection in Humanitarian Action (ALNAP 2018), where relevant.

The OECD DAC updated evaluation criteria and a guidance note accompanying it can be found at: https://www.oecd.org/dac/evaluation/daccriteriaforevaluatingdevelopmentassistance.htm

The evaluation criteria are also a useful tool for maintaining the evaluation's focus and utility once the evaluation questions have been generated. The criteria are especially helpful when consolidating or drawing thematic or operational lessons from a number of evaluation reports.

A good starting place in establishing the evaluation's criteria are the OECD DAC criteria (table 2.1), although not all may be relevant or appropriate to incorporate. Evaluation managers and evaluators should instead focus on those criteria most relevant to the evaluation's purpose and intended use, or conduct an in-depth analysis of a few of them. For example, it may be difficult to attribute impact to a specific intervention in an FCV setting; therefore the evaluation focus in this regard could relate to the intervention's intended or unintended longer-term results. The same reasoning applies in measuring sustainability.

Table 2.1 **OECD DAC criteria and corresponding overarching questions**

Criterion	Question
Relevance	Are we doing the right things?
Coherence	How well does the intervention fit?
Effectiveness	Are we achieving our objectives?
Efficiency	Are we making best use of resources?
Impact	Are we making a difference (positive and negative, direct and indirect, intended and unintended change)?
Sustainability	Will its benefits last over the long term once the intervention has ended?

Source: OECD DAC 2019.
Note: Gender and conflict sensitivity should be embedded throughout.

The OECD DAC evaluation criteria set the international standards for an evaluation. Sometimes, evaluation designers may feel pressured to include all six criteria, but ultimately the evaluation scope and available resources should determine which criteria are, and are not, included in the evaluation design. Appropriate prioritization can be achieved through discussions between the evaluation commissioners and the evaluators. Using these standard OECD DAC criteria makes meta-evaluation – the drawing of lessons from a wide range of evaluations – much easier. Also, standard criteria are likely to capture common weaknesses in humanitarian action based on experience and research (ALNAP 2016).

There is always a risk that interventions will have positive or negative unintended effects. If these are known prior to the evaluation, they should be explicitly incorporated into its design. Otherwise, the evaluation can help reveal what those unintended effects might be (see box 2.1). The World Food Programme includes a broad evaluation question on unintended effects in its evaluation terms of reference to allow evaluators to explore this. Where possible and appropriate, unintended effects once identified can be measured both quantitatively and qualitatively.

DESIGN EVALUATION QUESTIONS

Evaluation questions help focus the evaluation work on key issues, thus allowing for better reflection on the evaluation criteria, more targeted data collection, more in-depth analysis and a more useful evaluation overall (Independent Evaluation Office of IFAD 2015).

The evaluation questions are typically developed by the evaluation managers in coordination with the evaluation reference group to define what an evaluation exercise seeks to answer. The types of questions will determine what information will be gathered and the methodology required to collect this information. In FCV situations, the evaluation questions should be conflict- and gender-sensitive and be designed taking into account their impact on methodology, time and other resources. Considering the challenges around access and data gathering in FCV contexts, it is useful to keep the number of evaluation questions to as few as possible – on a "need to know" basis rather than "good to know". Having too many questions defined for an evaluation exercise may mean, beyond the safety and security challenges posed to the people being evaluated and the evaluators, that the evaluation just scratches the surface rather than provides an in-depth analysis of what works in such complex and sometime volatile contexts.

Each selected evaluation criteria should have an overarching question (as shown in table 2.1) and a set of sub-questions tailored to and informing the pathways in the theory of change.

In formulating the evaluation questions:

For more on formulating evaluation questions, see the European Commission's Capacity4dev wiki: https://europa.eu/capacity4dev/evaluation_guidelines/wiki/preparing-evaluation-question-0

- Use straightforward, plain language.
- Make specific reference to the intervention(s) to be evaluated.
- Construct a clear hypothesis that can be tested within the evaluation.
- Clearly relate the question to the evidence base and address a known gap in the evidence.
- Define the target group within the question.

CONSTRUCT THE EVALUATION FRAMEWORK

The evaluation framework is the core of the evaluation design. Its purpose is to ensure that evaluators clearly establish the links among the various elements underpinning the design of the evaluation that have been explored in this step: the evaluation criteria, questions, indicators and targets as well as the quantitative and qualitative research tools for primary data collection. The purpose is to establish a clear evidence trail to support findings (Independent Evaluation Office of IFAD 2015); for this reason, the framework is presented in matrix form.

Construction and piloting

The following checklist, adapted from CDA Collaborative (2017), is useful in constructing an FCV evaluation framework and piloting the evaluation locally.

Read more about the do no harm principle on this page of the Conflict Sensitivity Consortium and refer to this Do No Harm Checklist of the CDA Collaborative.

- Do the evaluation questions prioritize the identification of unintended effects, both positive and negative?
- Are the evaluation questions gender- and conflict-sensitive and designed to do no harm?
- Is the evaluation framework itself gender- and conflict-sensitive and designed to do no harm? For example, does it consider how data collection can avoid fuelling tensions and putting affected people/communities at risk? Will the act of asking questions cause suspicion, rumours or fear? If focus group discussions are to be used, would it be better to meet with different ethnic/religious groups separately to avoid clashes of opinion over disputed events or results? Alternatively, would meeting together help reduce divisions and ease mutual suspicions by ensuring transparency? Is sampling based on consensual targeting criteria for all affected groups with data collectors from the same community and tools specifically designed for that particular group? Are the evaluation team or enumerators viewed as acceptable/

trustworthy by target communities? Do the team/enumerators have the capacity to take in all perspectives equitably?

- Does the evaluation framework prioritize participants' physical and emotional security and the security of their data, dignity and reputation? Does it foresee how certain behaviours or actions (e.g. the use of armed escorts) can foster mistrust or make the evaluation team a target? Does it draw on local knowledge of partners and staff operating on the ground, building in mechanisms that allow for flexibility?
- Does the evaluation framework consider the unintended effects, both positive and negative, of the intervention and evaluation activities and their impact on the environment? Does the sampling strategy take into consideration methods to minimize environmental impact – e.g. hiring local consultants over international consultancies to reduce the impacts of transportation, conducting mobile surveys rather than paper-based surveys to reduce printing, and prioritizing online products for dissemination rather than printed reports?

The OECD DAC criteria implicitly call for investing time and resources in assessment of unintended effects (OECD DAC 2019).

Unintended consequences

Following are a few actions that will allow the evaluation team to ensure that the evaluation framework accounts for the unintended consequences of an intervention:

- Include assessment of unintended effects in the evaluation design.
- Adaptive management actions undertaken during intervention implementation should inform the evaluation design. Monitoring results has proven to be beneficial in tapping into the unintended consequences of an intervention, and support adaptive management, (Blommestein et al. 2018; see box 2.1). If unintended effects of an intervention are identified during implementation, interventions can be adapted quickly to minimize harm and maximize benefits. This learning-as-you-go approach is at the core of developmental evaluation, where learning from evaluative thinking – focusing on how desired results/changes/outcomes are affected – informs adaptation, practice and decision-making.

Considering the above, it is useful to collect examples of how monitoring data supported adaptive programming by informing decision makers – especially if these resulted in timely intervention fixes. These examples will provide

Box 2.1 **Evaluating unintended effects and adaptive management in Pakistan**

In Pakistan, Community World Service Asia and Y Care International set an example of evaluating unintended effects and adaptive management by incorporating outcome harvesting in their monitoring frameworks. The agencies established locally owned monitoring tools and community feedback mechanisms by creating local project steering groups and a mobile phone–based feedback mechanism using Frontline SMS software. In the final evaluation, it was found that the project was adapted towards dealing with both positive and negative unintended effects and their consequences. For example, the steering group settled a potential conflict between women entrepreneurs and landlords by providing more men to work in the fields to counterbalance the drop in female workers caused by their finding alternative work.

Source: Blommestein et al. 2018.

an understanding of the intervention's unintended effects and show how well the intervention was managed.

Where possible, the evaluation commissioners and development interventions programmers could think of adaptive management in an intervention with a focus on evaluation. This would simply mean introducing approaches that build in evaluation to the intervention from the beginning: the idea is to do a bit of work, then evaluate it and test if it works, and adapt based on the results. The evaluation commissioners and intervention designers could look more to integrating evaluation – especially nimble (low cost and rapid) evaluations – throughout the programme to enable the test-and-adapt model. Evaluations done in adaptive management programmes can be used as a good source of evidence for any mid-term or final evaluation as well as monitoring.

Flexibility and the evaluation framework

Interventions in FCV contexts may start out without a clear design; they may build in regular monitoring and evaluation techniques to test and define the approach and work as they go along. To enhance learning in such complex scenarios, it is useful to assess the extent to which the intervention was adapted to remain relevant to the context – both rapidly changing ones, and protracted and slow-burning conflicts. Include the following questions in the evaluation framework:

- Did the intervention team set flexible but realistic goals?
- Were these goals revised with relevant stakeholders if the conflict dynamics changed?
- Was the donor understanding and flexible?
- Was the monitoring locally owned?
- Were the monitoring tools and resources adapted to meet real-time needs on the ground, if needed?
- Was an enabling environment for learning developed in the intervention?
- Did the intervention monitor trends in gender- and protection-related risks, e.g. by tracking increases/decreases in forced recruitment to armed forces, sexual violence and domestic violence?
- Were local communities or affected populations involved in monitoring activities?
- Did the intervention establish strong beneficiary feedback mechanisms to ensure accountability to the affected population? How was the feedback analysed and used to assess the interaction between the intervention and the conflict, and vice versa? How were they used to ensure accountability to the affected populations? How inclusive were the feedback mechanisms?
- Did the intervention and monitoring and evaluation staff have the necessary skills to work in an FCV context?

TAILOR METHODS AND TOOLS

In FCV contexts, evaluators are required to develop flexible and adaptive evaluation strategies to meet the needs of a constantly changing environment and of slow-burning conflicts, protracted conflicts or crises. These tools must be tailored and sensitive to a fluid context. The following are key points for evaluators and evaluation commissioners to consider in planning and implementing an effective and useful evaluation.

Use mixed methods

Use a range of qualitative and quantitative evaluation methods and sources. Where possible and appropriate, use data collection methods such as **beneficiary surveys**, **focus group discussions**, and **structured and semi-structured interviews** with intervention stakeholders. Data should be disaggregated by sex, age and other protected characteristics to the extent possible; where possible, probe deeper into aspects of intersectionality, including gender roles and power relations as identified by the gender and conflict analysis. In some cases, data can also be disaggregated by conflict identity group.

In FCV contexts or when access to communities is limited, as with the current COVID-19 pandemic, **information and communication technologies (ICTs)** can offer reasonable alternatives in the absence of face-to-face interviews in FCV contexts – e.g. via mobile phone/tablet-based surveys, and the use of drones for evaluation purposes. Moreover, remote sensing, geographic information system (GIS) mapping, meteorological and economic data, and big data made available through different sources can be extremely useful when it is not possible to carry out field missions for primary data collection. Where possible and reliable, consider administrative data – i.e., data produced by official government authorities and surveys done by other companies, governments or organizations.

See Step 5 for more information, tips and guidance on using ICTs.

Align evaluation design and methods with the kind of evaluation being done

Understanding the design and implementation of the intervention under evaluation is a key factor in developing an appropriate evaluation design. Especially for evaluations in an FCV context, this understanding is crucial for testing the assumptions underlying the theory of change about how development interventions affect change, which is in turn important for understanding the results on the ground (Gaarder and Annan 2013).

Experimental and **quasi-experimental** design options for impact evaluation and its variations such as **factorial design**, **pipeline approach**, **pair-matched randomization** and **double difference** have proven to be useful in evaluations in FCV contexts (Puri et al. 2015). Non-experimental design impact evaluation approaches also can be useful; these can integrate qualitative methods such as **theory-based evaluation**, **contribution**

analysis, **process tracing** and **qualitative comparative analysis**. Depending on the situation, newer methods for data collection and analysis such as **predictive analytics** and **satellite imagery** might be appropriate in FCV contexts (Hassnain 2019b).

Note that emergent, goal-free evaluation approaches such as outcome harvesting and most significant change can be well suited to identifying unintended effects.

In addition to these more traditional evaluation methods are the learning-oriented methods listed in table 2.2. If time, resources or volatility in the context does not allow for traditional methods, use one or a mix of these learning methods to generate knowledge and initiate processes of organizational learning.

In designing the evaluation approach:

- Ask whether the methods are ethically acceptable; realistic; appropriate to the context; conflict-, climate- and gender-sensitive; and respectful of the do no harm principle.
- Aim to implement the best and tested evaluation approaches for the affected population rather than experimenting.

Use participatory methods

For more on participatory methods, see the guide written for UNICEF on "Participatory Approaches" (Gujit 2014): https://www.unicef-irc.org/publications/pdf/brief_5_participatoryapproaches_eng.pdf

Also see Hassnain's blogpost on engaging children through the evaluation cycle: https://gendereval.ning.com/profiles/blogs/children-measuring-their-perceived-level-of-safety-in-fragile-and

When evaluating in FCV contexts, access to local communities may be restricted or impossible in light of security issues. Access is also likely to be limited during pandemic situations. Notwithstanding these challenges, the views of all stakeholder groups – including refugees and internally displaced people – should be incorporated to the extent possible in the design, conduct and dissemination of the evaluation.

The use of informed participatory evaluation that engages all stakeholders of an intervention or policy in the process is encouraged to best capture the effects on different individuals and groups. Informed participation is often key to the identification and analysis of unintended effects, both positive and negative. However, the evaluator must walk a fine line between constrained and transparent informed participation. Maintaining this balance requires integrity, experience, flexibility and leadership in order to plan and ensure safe and meaningful involvement and a secure environment for all parties. It also requires an objective but respectful understanding of the particular culture, because when resources are being distributed and information shared, a range of sociocultural norms come into play which might superficially be considered irrelevant in the particular context. For example, the concept of "honour" in an honour-prone society could trigger discussions on justified distributions and the exclusion of particular groups.

Note that in insecure environments, the involvement of local communities could raise a range of security and ethical issues – as well as increased expectations among participating stakeholders with regard to new interventions, funding, benefits, etc. A well-planned and thoughtful process is required to manage these concerns and ensure safe and meaningful involvement.

Table 2.2 **Learning-oriented evaluation methods and tools**

Method	Description	Comments
After-action review (AAR)	AAR is a facilitated process enabling those involved in an intervention to reflect on what happened, challenges and learning. It can be used at the end of an intervention or during its implementation.	If it is not feasible to have an external and/or independent evaluation, an AAR can be facilitated by the evaluator to capture learning and capitalize on it for future interventions.
Most significant change (MSC)	MSC is a tool for collecting, discussing and selecting stories about the changes people experience as a result of an intervention. People discussing the change stories themselves select the most significant story. MSC is not intended as a stand-alone methodology but should be combined with other evaluation methods such as short surveys and focus group discussions.	Like many research methods, MSC has certain limitations and biases. These include biases towards success stories, popular views and people with good storytelling skills. MSC raises the important issue of voice/power associated with who participated in the story selection process.
Outcome harvesting (OH)	OH collects (harvests) evidence on outcomes and then, working backwards, determines whether and how an intervention has contributed to these changes.	OH requires high-quality skills and a long time span to identify and formulate outcome descriptions. Only those outcomes informants are aware of are captured. The participation of those who influenced the outcomes is crucial. Starting with outcomes and working backwards represents a new way of thinking about change for some participants. An evaluator needs to take extra steps to prevent the risk of bias and overestimation of outcomes and an intervention's contribution to these outcomes.
Real-time evaluation (RTE)	The primary objective of RTE is to provide feedback in a participatory way in real time (i.e. during the evaluation fieldwork) to those executing and managing the intervention or the humanitarian response.	If the context is rapidly changing, consider conducting an RTE to provide quick feedback during the life of the intervention or during evaluation field work. RTE can be costly.
Developmental evaluation (DE)	DE unfolds in complex dynamic systems where the particular meaning and significance of information may be difficult to predetermine. Making sense of emergent findings involves evaluators' interpreting patterns in the data collaboratively with social innovators, funders, advocates, change agents and system change supporters. DE provides evaluative information and feedback to social innovators, and their funders and supporters, to inform adaptive development of change initiatives in complex dynamic environments (Patton, McKegg and Wehipeihana 2016).	DE empowers those working together towards common goals to embed evaluative thinking in the work they do and share their learning in order to inform next steps (Kuji-Shikatani et al. 2016). DE provides accountability for funders and supporters of social innovation, and helps them understand and refine their contributions to solutions as they evolve. Evaluators require deep understanding and skills in a wide range of methodological competencies so as to be creatively responsive in the face of complexity (Patton, McKegg and Wehipeihana 2016).

Obtain informed consent

Seek to obtain informed consent – and, ideally, multiple informed consent (where consent is received at different stages of a process; see box 2.1) – from all stakeholders prior to engaging them in evaluation activities and before collecting any information related to them. This measure is especially vital when collecting any personal information or identifiable material such as photos/videos. Many organizations have their own protocol as to how to request consent; become familiar with this protocol, or – in its absence – seek tools and guidance on best practice from other organizations.

Informed consent means telling individuals about the evaluation and asking them whether they are willing to participate. In most cases, the evaluation team will need to prepare an informed consent form to be reviewed and signed by participants prior to their involvement in any part of the evaluation. This form gives the evaluation team written permission to use information from that participant in reports and presentations. Consent should be regarded as an ongoing process, and it should be made clear to participants that they are free to withdraw their consent or ask for further information at any point in time (SPA 2009).

In FCV contexts, informed consent becomes even more crucial, given the considerations around participants' safety and how and with whom they can share data (box 2.1). And on their part, people might not understand where their information goes or what is meant by sharing consolidated evaluation findings through the Internet. It is advisable to aim for multiple consent processes in communities to ensure comprehension on all sides.

Communicate directly with participants

The I-DEAL monitoring and evaluation Toolkit developed by War Child Holland is a useful source that can be adapted to the particular context and individuals you are working with – even of a different age: https://www.warchildholland.org/projects/i-deal/

Regardless of the analytical method(s) selected, understanding people's perception of change in FCV environments is vital, as such contexts are politically complex, different groups are affected differently by crises, and it is hard to assume a direct causal relationship between context and intervention. Additionally, peace or cohesion may mean different things and have different value to different people. Wherever it is feasible, verbal, face-to-face communication is essential to perceiving these nuances. Moreover, people tend to be more forthcoming and frank when addressed in person, as opposed to having to provide feedback to an unseen interrogator over the telephone or in writing on a questionnaire – an option that might not be viable at all when working with participants of low literacy. The evaluator must work without passing judgement, relying on active listening and empathetic understanding.

Take extra care to triangulate the sources of perceptions. Perceptions need to be elicited from people on all key sides of the conflict or difference at hand.

Box 2.2 **Case study: Informed consent for participatory evaluation activities in Bangladesh, Pakistan and Thailand**

An international non-governmental organization (NGO) working with disadvantaged children in three refugee contexts – settlements in Thailand and Pakistan and closed camps in Bangladesh – brought evaluators in to conduct a participatory photography baseline evaluation. The aim was to gain an understanding of child participation in play while exploring child protection issues and disaster risk reduction.

The ways in which informed consent was obtained for evaluation activities differed in each context, and no clear protocol was followed – regardless of whether it existed.

For example, in the settlements in Thailand, staff supporting refugees always asked parents for consent before allowing children under age 18 to participate in evaluation activities. Parents did not know exactly what they were consenting to, just that their children would be participating in an evaluation activity. Recognizing that true informed consent cannot be granted until the outputs of an evaluation activity can be seen, the evaluators pushed for a multiple consent process. Parents were asked to give consent prior to their children participating in evaluation activities (in this case a workshop); they were also invited to attend a photo exhibition when the evaluation outputs (photos) were ready. Upon viewing the photos, parents could give consent for their use for different purposes.

As a long-standing good practice, photos including unidentifiable children can be used for multiple purposes; but if children can be identified, it is extremely important to obtain consent before the photo is used further. The 2018 implementation of the European General Data Protection Regulation makes this practice a legal requirement within Europe. Outside of Europe, however, each country has its own regulations in this regard, and organisations need to respect and adhere to these. The evaluators were working for a global organization, so there was a strong need to push for better practice. The new consent process was supported by local staff who were keen to adapt their evaluation practices to improve their ways of working.

Pakistan presented a different context, since communities had been in settlements for a long time. The local community-based NGO partnering with the international NGO was reluctant to change its ways of working in asking parents for consent. Local staff were responsible for requesting consent; they were aware of good practice, but faced challenges with the local NGO partners.

In Bangladesh and Thailand photo exhibitions to obtain final consent were held publicly. In contrast, due to safety concerns, the exhibition in Pakistan was only open for parents and children. Extra precautions were taken to ensure that no one was put at risk.

This evaluation exercise demonstrated that there are different ways of understanding and putting ethical considerations into practice. Obtaining a signed consent form before an evaluation activity takes place is not sufficient on its own, because people do not know what they are consenting to until they see a final product. The multiple consent process can be applied to various evaluation activities where informed consent is required.

Source: Interviews with Soledad Muñiz, InsightShare.

Accept challenges to rigour and the probable lack of a counterfactual

See the ALNAP resource on strengthening the quality of evidence: https://www.alnap.org/help-library/strengthening-the-quality-of-evidence-in-humanitarian-evaluations

Good-quality, credible evidence is key to the success of any intervention but is of special value in FCV settings. In such contexts, there are a variety of competing stakeholders and users who may not agree on the outcomes – in conflict settings, even peace may mean different things for different stakeholders. At the same time, defining "good-quality" and "credible", setting up the hierarchy of results and identifying the counterfactuals are key challenges in these highly insecure and conflict-affected settings. This may mean that the approach to gathering and sharing evidence may be different than in normal settings.

See the Qualitative Impact Protocol (QUIP) for alternative ways of establishing counterfactuals or attributing change in an FCV context: https://www.bath.ac.uk/projects/evaluating-social-and-development-interventions-using-the-qualitative-impact-protocol-quip/

In FCV situations, challenges to methodological and evaluative rigour can – in fact, must – be accepted as part of the flexibility that characterizes successful approaches to working in highly insecure settings.

Avoid conflict of interest/bias

An evaluator should never tolerate any form of bias that skews the evaluation significantly towards the perspective of one side of the conflict and away from another. Evaluators must not take partisan positions and should maintain a position of neutrality. Adherence to this principle is critical in FCV settings because there are multiple definitions of and perspectives on what change (e.g. peace) is; it can be perceived differently within and across countries and regions; different actors have different interests and may choose different things to monitor and measure. Above all, it is important to understand that data gathered, or their possible interpretations, may not be neutral in FCV contexts.

Tips for avoiding bias include the following:

- Ensure that all key sides in and perspectives on a conflict are included as much as possible when identifying evaluation stakeholders, team members and participants/informants. It may not be easy to determine which key groups or perspectives are required, so consult with a diverse range of local colleagues and long-term expatriates who know the context well.
- Explore critically the positioning and reputation of the implementing agency and the donor within the context. Do people within the context view them as even-handed and unbiased? Are they equally respected and accepted by all identity groups within the context, or do some groups view them differently than others? What are the implications for the intervention itself and for the evaluation?
- Always consult the legitimate internationally recognized government, but do not uncritically accept all government data or perspectives. In FCV environments, governments may not be positioned neutrally, which might lead to a bias – intentional or unintentional – in their reporting. In cases of de facto authorities,

identify their data sources and their authenticity before quoting the data or information in evaluation findings.

- Team members should sign a conflict of interest form stating their independence from intervention and their commitment to maintain neutrality.

Data collection field visit at the Inaa Guxa minefield in Somaliland. Photo: Jess Rice

Step 3: **Select the Evaluation Team**

In all evaluation environments, selecting the right evaluation team is critical in ensuring the independence and reliability of information and the overall credibility of the evaluation. In FCV contexts, choosing the right people and institutions carries even greater weight, as alliances and loyalties in such settings can change swiftly. Be careful not to default to familiar people or institutions, but commit time and effort to carefully ensuring that the appropriate team members or partners are selected.

An evaluation team made up of members with complementary skills suitable to the task ahead is recommended. Planners and commissioners should specify the required competencies in the evaluation terms of reference and, if relevant, in the tender documents. Particular attention should be given to the perception of bias in the team, and an understanding of conflict sensitivity and gender, among other evaluation-related skills (OECD 2012).

The World Food Programme's experience in attracting senior, experienced evaluators in FCV contexts is varied. Often evaluators are unwilling to take on these assignments unless directly hired by the World Food Programme with enhanced security guarantees. Thus, while it is important not to default to familiar personnel, it is difficult to broaden the pool of evaluators willing to travel to Yemen, Syria or the Democratic Republic of Congo. One way around this is to plan and search for the team well ahead of time, earlier than one would normally do.

CONSIDERATIONS IN SELECTING THE EVALUATION TEAM OR PARTNERS

In addition to the usual requirements for a solid evaluation team – including team members with solid research/evaluation skills and ensuring a balanced mix of genders – the following considerations apply to FCV contexts.

- **International staff.** Using international staff may affect the way in which the evaluation team is perceived and treated and their access to information. Be aware of the individual's/institution's ethnic, religious, socioeconomic and political affiliations. For international teams, ascertain nationality beforehand. When hiring staff for and from the conflict-affected regions or conflicting groups, take their personal safety risks into consideration, as well as any threats their involvement may incur to the rest of the evaluation team and to the credibility of the evaluation itself. The risk of the team being perceived as biased, or of them not being given access to certain information, should also be weighed. Any implications for data collection or analysis should be identified and addressed.
- **Local and national consultants.** Do they have the trust of the communities with which they will be working? Are there any recent or ongoing hostilities between the individual/institution and local or national authorities, communities, political or other groups? Ask direct and indirect stakeholders, as widely as possible.

See Step 1 for more information on conducting a conflict analysis.

- **Conflict analysis orientation.** Ensure the individual/institution is committed to, and can see the benefits of, the evaluation team conducting a level of conflict analysis.
- **Conflict sensitivity.** Have informal discussions around conflict and crisis sensitivity to gauge the individual's/institution's perspectives on conflict-sensitive principles.
- **Bias.** Critically reflect on the individual's/institution's perception and analysis of the conflict to identify any bias.
- **Affiliations.** Where does the individual/organization get its financial resources? Ensuring no formal or informal affiliation to any party to the conflict is critical – and challenging – in FCV environments.
- **Principles.** Discuss the individual's/organization's knowledge of, and experience with, conflict sensitivity and do no harm, protection and humanitarian principles.

ENSURING TEAM SAFETY

Once the evaluation team has been identified and recruited, ensuring their safety is extremely important. For local evaluators, this safety becomes part of the duty of care of their employer organization/consulting firm (if any). In most cases, organizations commissioning the evaluation, especially donors, do not accept or hold the duty of care for contractors/evaluation teams; and the contracting organization arranges its own security. Although it is a separate policy-level debate, to avoid any harm to the communities being evaluated, every evaluation commissioner should hold or share at least some responsibility for the safety and security of the people involved in an evaluation or at least ensure that the contracting companies have appropriate duty of care arrangements in place.

See Step 4 for more on safely conducting primary data collection.

Evaluations in FCV contexts may require direct contact with affected populations in collecting data through focus group discussions, in-depth interviews or surveys. These typical evaluation data collection exercises can, in volatile locations, be dangerous for the local evaluation team. As discussed in the preceding steps, the risks of evaluation – especially of primary data collection – to evaluators and communities should be assessed well in advance and reflected in the evaluation approaches and tools. These risks should be mitigated through a risk assessment plan. Risk analysis should be done to identify the potential risks, assess its impact and probability, come up with an overall risk rating, then conduct risk mitigation (box 3.1).

TIPS FOR ENSURING THE SAFETY OF THE EVALUATION TEAM

An evaluator must understand that no accountability measures or requirements supersede the safety of the people – those who are collecting the data, the respondents and the evaluands. Many organizations will have their own specific security protocols; however, the following are some key principles that should be followed while designing or commissioning an evaluation in FCV environments to avoid harm to the local evaluation team.

- Evaluation commissioning agencies, firms and/or team leaders should ensure where possible that all members have been certified online and/or through field security training. Some certification training resources include the United Nations' mandatory Safe and Secure Approaches in Field Environments (SSAFE) and the Norwegian Refugee Council's Hostile Environment Awareness Training (HEAT); specialized training is also available on situational awareness, first aid, kidnapping and hostage taking, illegal roadblocks, etc. These trainings can be expensive, so a discussion should be held with all parties involved in the commissioning of the evaluation to ensure duty of care. Adding adequate training as a key requirement in the terms of reference or contracting documents would highlight their importance to evaluation firms/consultants.
- Prior to starting evaluation fieldwork, the evaluation team should seek a security briefing from the organization(s) implementing the intervention being evaluated. Often, this information will help in assessing the feasibility of carrying out the envisaged evaluation; for instance, it may reveal that it would be too risky to conduct the evaluation as scheduled and activities might be better postponed to a later stage. Conversely, the briefing may confirm that the evaluation can take place as planned.
- If the fieldwork is deemed safe to pursue, the evaluation team should be accompanied by a local team member who is familiar with the political, security and physical landscape.
- The team should ensure it has access to relevant safety equipment, including satellite phones and service, emergency phone numbers (including of local enforcement agencies); medical supplies and know-how; and other tools to ensure safety in the event of a crisis (cash, source of battery-operated electricity, non-perishable food stuffs, water, etc.) as appropriate to the context.
- Evaluators need to guard their own safety when operating in an environment of active conflict or violence. They should always interface with local authorities or security professionals when venturing out into dangerous communities.
- Exercise caution when making any decisions about the presence of armed escorts in high-risk contexts. Despite the apparent benefits, armed escorts can in some contexts make the evaluation team more of a target.

Box 3.1 **Example: Why conducting a risk analysis makes a difference**

After emergency assistance and recovery support were provided following the 2018 Papua New Guinea (PNG) earthquake, development partners needed to hand-pick evaluation teams suited to the fragile operating context. Many international relief workers who were not familiar with the fragile environment incorrectly assumed that foreign development workers would be able to operate safely in the remote and rural beneficiary communities.

This proved not to be the case, however. Early discussions and rapid fragility analysis with those familiar with that part of PNG would have identified the heightened safety risks from the outset. Evidencing the severity of the risk to evaluation teams, early UNICEF mission teams (including staff) were directly exposed to life-threatening attacks on several occasions. UNICEF deployed staff to what they now, in hindsight, define as an active conflict zone – with almost no operational presence, few implementing partners on the ground, and limited prior experience in dealing with a large-scale humanitarian emergency in the region.

For a discussion of the use of armed escorts, see the World Food Programme's 2018 publication, "Evaluation of WFP Policies on Humanitarian Principles and Access in Humanitarian Contexts: https://www1.wfp.org/publications/wfps-policies-humanitarian-principles-and-access-humanitarian-contexts-policy-evaluation-ter

Heightened security in post-conflict Colombia observed during an evaluation mission. Photo: Anupam Anand

PHASE B

Conducting the Evaluation

Two internally displaced girls from the Yazidi community in Iraq are returning to their camp after participating in a focus group discussion. Photo: Hur Hassnain

Step 4: Organize a Field Mission for Data Collection

Evaluations in contexts of fragility, conflict and violence (FCV) need to ensure that all stakeholders agree with the activities to be undertaken in conducting the evaluation. Evaluators should conduct a scoping mission to engage with key stakeholders to define and clarify the evaluation details and, as necessary, pilot test tools. By so doing, unintended consequences can be addressed – especially any that may endanger vulnerable stakeholders and the evaluation team members themselves (Fan 2016; World Bank 2017).

This guidance about conducting a scoping mission also applies to evaluations proposed in contexts that are difficult to reach (e.g. because of geographical location or pandemic/crisis situation).

GATHERING DATA IN FCV CONTEXTS

As mentioned in phase A, the evaluation team, in most cases, could benefit from applying a mixed-methods approach and nuanced tools to gather the most suitable and contextualized data to support a rigorous analysis.

The data collection process should take into account factors that go beyond those that may have an immediate impact on the intervention being evaluated – including political, military, social and economic factors that may lie outside the scope of the intervention, but may become relevant given the rapidly changing context. Moreover, rigorous evaluations should draw on accurate, relevant data on women, men and gender relations. The inclusion of such data can help to ensure that evaluations are gender- and conflict-sensitive, makes gender disparities more visible, and can assist in answering the evaluation questions.

Prolonged violence and situations of high tension can pose significant data availability problems that often restrict evaluators' work. For example, it may not be possible to locate certain intervention beneficiaries (or other relevant stakeholders) because they are in prison, deceased or otherwise unavailable. The evaluation must account for such data gaps and explain in its reporting how these missing data/sources have been compensated for (OECD 2012).

COLLECTING PRIMARY DATA

Primary data can be collected through surveys that are prepared during the evaluation design and piloted in the field.

To gather data in FCV contexts, the evaluator should develop and make available a conflict-sensitive evaluation protocol that is informed by an ethical human research design.

Surveys should be secure and responses anonymous as much as possible. Depending on the level of sensitivity in the specific evaluation context, an external actor – third-party monitor, call centre, think tank, university – can be engaged to conduct the work "unbranded". Consult with development actors working in this location for advice, such as experts involved in security management, peacebuilding actors, etc. In any event, carefully assess the most appropriate method/tool for conducting the survey.

Hiring local evaluators or data collectors

Hiring local evaluators and enumerators can have several advantages in terms of cost reduction and access to communities and information. However, deploying local people for evaluation in FCV environments can entail risk and raise some ethical concerns. Make sure to consider all possible risks and develop mitigation strategies for each scenario. Be mindful that the safety of people will always take precedence over the desire for accountability to senior management, donors, taxpayers etc., and the collection of data.

Non-local enumerators and other personnel conducting qualitative studies should also be protected. Enumerators must be trained on safety procedures and have access to support. Insurance policies should be in place to cover all eventualities.

Involving local people in data collection

See the World Food Programme's Guidance on remote mobile technology for household food security data collection and using private sector and call centres for data collection: https://resources.vam.wfp.org/mVAM

Local intervention participants have an interest in seeing interventions delivered successfully. Therefore, if it can be done safely, involve local intervention beneficiaries and other stakeholders in data collection. If designed sensitively, this can be both good practice from a participation perspective and a practical way of collecting data. One way to accomplish this is through establishing reference groups consisting of local community members, state duty bearers and civil society and involve them in assessing outputs and outcomes.

Having communities collect evaluation data is useful in many contexts, but it may also raise questions of evaluation independence as community participants may often be intervention beneficiaries.

Interviews

In conducting interviews in FCV contexts, pay careful attention to the following.

What questions are asked. Questions posed should be sufficiently general that they are impartial, but specific enough to obtain the data needed. Collect non-political data, and then triangulate these using open sources whenever possible, as this can reduce the risk for both the interviewer and the interviewee.

How the questions are asked. Decide whether any conflict-related questions unrelated to the intervention are being asked, and how that data will be used. Allow the interviewee to go "off the record" if needed and to apply the Chatham House rule – i.e. that any information used from the interview withholds the speaker's identity and affiliation. In normal circumstances, off the record data cannot be used as evaluation data for reasons of transparency. In FCV contexts, anonymous source data can be reported for the security and safety of both the respondents and the data gatherers in compliance with strict confidentiality provisions and data protection measures.

- Be aware that discussions about drivers of conflict and other conflict-sensitive issues can be emotional and political. Eliciting this information will take more time than addressing less charged subject matter and will likely entail building trust.
- Manage interviewees' expectations. These difficult questions are being asked in the context of evaluation and may not result in a change or assistance.

Refer to Step 1 and Step 2 for more detail on how to engage with people or institutions in FCV contexts.

Who asks the questions and of whom. In an FCV context, no one is truly neutral. Take into account age, political affiliation, ethnic and religious identity, gender, etc., when sending interviewers to the affected population.

Who answers the questions. In an FCV context, always remember that talking to someone – regardless of the topic or responses – may pose a risk to the interviewee as well as the interviewer.

COLLECTING SECONDARY DATA

Primary data should be complemented with secondary data that can be obtained from a wide range of sources including, but not limited to, humanitarian, security and peacebuilding sector partners.

- Partners engaged in wide-scale medical or food distribution will have knowledge of evolving demographic and household patterns, as well as the political economy considerations required for distribution (e.g. the World Food Programme) or may have data on displacement (e.g. the United Nations Refugee Agency, the International Organization for Migration, UNICEF, the United Nations Population Fund). Several independent organizations – universities, research labs, think tanks, the private sector, etc. – are also curators of such databases.

- Partners engaged in the security sector (e.g. the United Nations Department of Safety and Security, the United Nations Office for the Coordination of Humanitarian Affairs) will have data on shifting areas of insecurity, roadblocks, checkpoints and control of assets.
- Non-governmental organizations will have data on grievances and perceived needs, including the needs of the most vulnerable, women and children.
- Partners working in peacebuilding or conflict prevention should have recent conflict analyses. They may also have conflict-sensitivity reports that help identify the context-specific operational risks of exacerbating tensions.
- Earth observation data from satellites can be leveraged to understand landscape dynamics. Satellite data can provide information on changes in housing patterns and agricultural practices, and identify settlement sites of internally displaced persons. Satellite images have helped identify sites such as damaged, burned and bulldozed human settlements in areas of conflict. This type of information can be crucial for areas that are difficult to access given their remote location or on-the-ground situation, and for corroborating other data sources. Broader context, and proxy data on socioeconomic and physical conditions, accessibility, etc., can also extracted from earth observation data. This is discussed further in Step 5.

Focus group discussion for an evaluation exercise with reformed warriors in Karamoja, Uganda.
Photo: Sabine Hellmann

Step 5: **Arrange Remote Data Collection**

There is growing use of digital tools for data collection throughout the intervention and evaluation life cycle; and this has influenced the ways in which information is gathered, analysed, reported on and shared. This step entails using information and communication technology (ICT) to collect data remotely in FCV situations. Because there is not much documented evidence on the efficiency and effectiveness of using ICT (Raftree and Bamberger 2014), and because there are myriad tools available, this section introduces these tools – with the caveat that the evaluator choose and use them wisely.

USE OF DIGITAL TOOLS IN EVALUATION

In FCV contexts and in pandemics, face-to-face meetings are often difficult to organize. ICT solutions can offer a convenient way to reach stakeholders without being exposed to potentially risky situations arising from armed conflict or natural disaster. Arguably the most accessible and widespread technology is **short message service** (SMS), or text messaging, via smart or mobile phones. If done properly, SMS-based surveys, along with simple phone interviews, are a great way to reduce risk to evaluators and respondents in insecure areas.

Other applications and advantages of ICTs include the following:

- Global Positioning System (GPS)–enabled devices can verify the location of the interviewer and interviewees, while electronic versions of surveys can ensure that questions are asked in the correct order and can include automatic consistency checks.
- Cost savings can accrue from replacing paper, and the elimination of manual data entry. This can help reduce the carbon footprint of evaluation activities, ensuring environmental sensitivity and enabling larger sample sizes to be managed.
- ICTs can play a helpful role in checking to ensure the right subjects were selected and interviewed, or that questions were asked correctly, in the right order and with the correct follow-ups. The use of ICTs in FCVs can eliminate the need to re-collect data

over and over, or to manually copy information from poorly legible manual entries to a digital format.

- ICTs have great potential in helping to include the voices of vulnerable and underrepresented groups, particularly those in FCV contexts, broadening the types and volume of data being collected. Increasing the variety of data sources can help overcome sample bias to an extent, deliver higher-quality data and improve understanding of intervention impact in FCV contexts.

Though ICTs hold huge potential for evaluations in general – and for FCV contexts in particular – in terms of convenience, consistency, scope and access, they also pose a variety of risks (box 5.1), including the risk of sensitive data falling into the wrong hands and the ability to geolocate surveyors and enumerators (Hassnain 2019a). Moreover, the ubiquity of some ICTs (e.g. smartphones) and the novelty of others (e.g. drones) may tempt evaluation commissioners and evaluators to rely on an inappropriate or untested ICT at the expense of ensuring the "basics" of monitoring and evaluation.

The validity of an evaluation's findings depends in large part on data quality. In this regard, the power unleashed by "big data" also needs to be taken into account. Big data is commonly distinguished by its volume, velocity and variety (Goodchild 2013). The sheer quantity of big data is so immense it cannot be fully managed by human interpreters. Instead, computers are taught to teach themselves (artificial intelligence) how to interpret patterns among billions of data points. For instance, smart algorithms can predict and follow flu outbreaks by sifting through social media postings, looking for words associated with "feeling under the weather".

The deluge of data produced by smartphones for evaluation purposes can also add up to the point where specialized statistical analysis is needed to produce readily interpretable information.

Box 5.1 **Challenges and risks of digital tools in FCV settings**

- Digital tools can be quite impersonal; some people prefer human interaction.
- Not everyone has a mobile device. In FCV contexts, those who have phones or tablets – or the requisite expertise to use them – are often better off financially or male; this can bias results towards elites and not take women sufficiently into account. Certain communities are also averse to using technology.
- Digital tools can lead to an overreliance on quantitative evaluation methods; ideally, quantitative and qualitative techniques should go hand-in-hand.
- Unfamiliarity with digital tools can lead to their use at the expense of good monitoring and evaluation practice – including loss of quality control measures, over-collection of data with little capacity to analyse or provide context, and the loss of the personal rapport and contextual understanding obtained from intervention visits and face-to-face interviews.
- Respondents may not understand, or may distrust, mobile devices. At the institutional level, governments or local (armed) groups might distrust such powerful tools, seeing them as a threat. Some governments have allowed the use of mobile devices, but not their GPS component. Other governments have used GPS coordinates to track citizen contact.
- Privacy and security concerns exist, particularly when enumerators or correspondents use their own devices.

Source: Raftree and Bamberger 2014.

With so much quantitative data, and untold ways of parsing it, an evaluator arguably needs even better **qualitative** insight, gained through classic evaluation techniques, to

Figure 5.1 **Tips for conducting remote monitoring and evaluation**

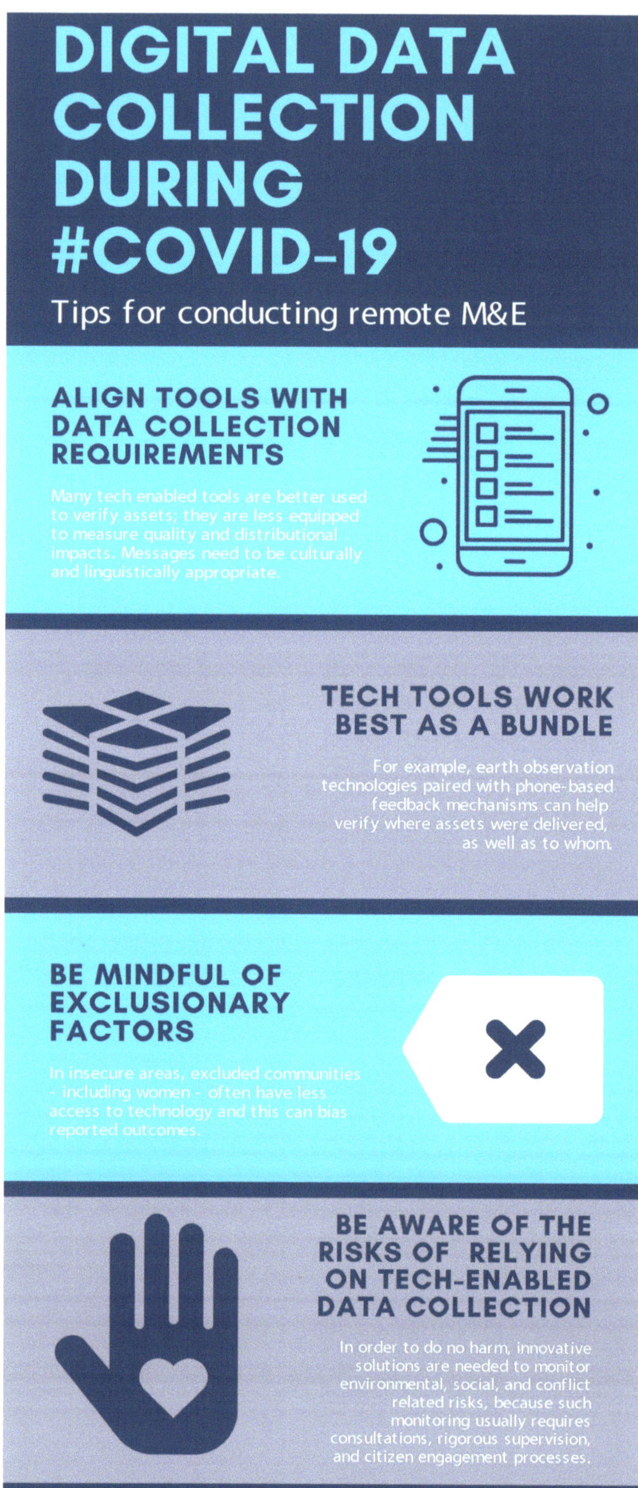

Source: Chelsky and Kelly 2020.

steer the analytical process in the right direction. In this regard, partnerships and collaboration between political, social and data scientists become critical (Hassnain 2019b).

In sum, an evaluator, especially one working in an insecure environment, must ensure that ICT use is a means and not an end. Chelsky and Kelly (2020), in the context of ICT use for COVID risk monitoring, point out that ICTs present many opportunities, but also limitations, in monitoring and evaluating development outcomes (figure 5.1); these must be considered when developing particular evaluation methods.

In unpredictable and complex contexts such as FCV and in pandemics, ICTs can offer creative solutions to compensate for the lack of face-to-face interaction. An evaluator needs to be aware of both the pros and cons of using ICTs for evaluation, especially in an FCV setting, as there can be risks and challenges associated with each method and tool. Table 5.1 presents a selection of ICT methods and tools, including their respective benefits and challenges.

HIGHLIGHT: SOME USEFUL AND INNOVATIVE ICT TOOLS AND TECHNIQUES

Evaluation in FCV situations means dealing with contexts that may be unpredictable, rapidly changing and sometimes violent. Using innovative and safe techniques can help in seeking the effects and their causes. The following are real-world examples of evaluating using a story-based method and by using geospatial analysis to make sense of data.

Story-based methods

Story-gathering/enquiry tools can be used to make sense of what happens in organizations and communities. Stories can be related to personal experiences, observations and situations.

Table 5.1 **ICT-based tools and techniques**

Description	Pros	Cons
Diary/journal logs		
In FCV settings, evaluation participants can complete a diary or journal log, which can be structured (like a questionnaire) or unstructured. Participants can record something every hour/day or when a certain change occurs. Different online platforms can be used; the logs can be visual (photo-based, collage, written) or spoken (voice recordings/memos). For more information, see https://www.betterevaluation.org/en/evaluation-options/logsanddiaries.	Can be combined with other interviews and methods; logs can be used as a prompt for further discussion. Can be used to document a range of data, usually making transparent a process or outcome or personal perspectives on how change occurred (Hyers 2018).	Requires access to the Internet; may also require access to a device that can take photos or record voice clips. Risk of selection bias: In some contexts, it might not be socially acceptable for women to participate; it might also exclude extremely poor people and refugees, internally displaced people or mobile populations.
Online interviews/discussions		
Online interviews can be conducted using audio-visual interfaces such as Skype, Zoom, Microsoft Teams, WebEx or GoToMeeting.	Enables audiovisual interactivity, including, for most platforms, via a chat box. Sessions can also be recorded for playback later.	Efforts need to be made to keep participants engaged in online conversations. People with no or poor Internet access/device may be excluded. This may include women, extremely poor, refugees, internally displaced people or mobile populations.
In **phone interviews**, a trained enumerator uses an interview script to guide discussion with a participant over the phone. For a list of available platforms, see https://mande.co.uk/2011/lists/software-lists/me-software-a-list/. For best practices and resources, see Kopper and Sautmann (2020).	Works well in contexts of low literacy. Can incorporate qualitative and quantitative questions. Usually provides richer data than SMS, interactive voice response and email surveys. Can achieve high response rates if well organized.	Requires respondents to have access to a phone/phone number and network coverage. More expensive than interactive voice response or SMS surveys. Requires high-quality enumerator training.
Focus group discussions can be conducted online where possible. The literature suggests that it is optimal to cap focus groups at around six participants (Daniels et al. 2019; Flynn, Albrecht and Scott 2018; Kite and Phongsavan 2017). For more information, see https://researchdesignreview.com/2020/03/16/focus-groups-moving-online-face-to-face-mode/.	In some cases, online groups can be "particularly well-suited" to deal with sensitive topics, and accessing an online venue can actually be less of a barrier to participation than carving out time to travel to a focus group facility (Forrestal, D'Angelo and Vogel 2015).	Online focus groups are prone to technology issues, lagging, Internet dropouts and interruptions. Only for people with Internet access and where it is socially acceptable; this may exclude women, extremely poor, refugees, internally displaced people or mobile populations.
Photo/video/voice elicitation		
Participants record observations of everyday practices and interactions to share with the evaluators. Questions or prompts can be provided in advance to guide the recordings, which are sent in photo, video and voice memo formats (Copes et al. 2018).	Less intrusive method of data collection. Participants share what they want to share. Allows for qualitative and quantitative responses. Can enable a connection between perceptions and observed activities.	Reviewing and coding photo, video or voice recording data can be labour-intensive. Requires participants to have access to a phone, camera or voice recorder and the means to send the recordings.

Description	Pros	Cons
Remote surveys		
Surveys can be administered remotely in many ways, as listed below. These offer convenient ways to reach stakeholders in hard-to-access areas and avoid exposure to risks arising from armed conflict, natural disasters or other obstacles. For more information, see Remote Survey Toolkit by 60 Decibels, https://60decibels.com/user/pages/03.Work/_remote_survey_toolkit/60_Decibels_Remote_Survey_Toolkit_March_2020.pdf.		
Interactive voice response (IVR) gives participants the option of responding to questions using a telephone touch pad (e.g. "What is your gender? For female, press 1. For male, press 2".). Using IVR, participants can be called directly or asked to call a toll-free phone number, enter a code and take the survey (Greenleaf and Vogel 2018). For more information, see https://www.viamo.io/wp-content/uploads/2018/07/Viamo-Brief-Data-Collection1595.pdf.	Low-cost method. Good for use in contexts where literacy levels are low and access to the Internet is limited. It easily accommodates language barriers and enables the collection of honest responses to sensitive questions.	Requires access to phone numbers or a creative way of sharing a toll-free phone number that can be dialled by participants. Requires access to a phone and network coverage, which entails the risk of selection bias.
There are several ways to administer **online surveys** remotely either through a weblink or from a mobile app. It is a low-cost method that allows for both qualitative and quantitative responses. Surveys can be sent en mass via email, and the survey can be longer than an SMS. Available options include but are not limited to KoBo Toolbox, SurveyMonkey, SurveyCTO, Google Forms, etc.	Participants have flexibility in responding to accommodate their own schedules. Has the potential to reach a large number of people.	Increased risk of selection bias. Requires respondents to have access to a smartphone/computer, excluding those without such access. Tends to have a low response rate. Also, lack of an interviewer to clarify questions might lead to inaccurate responses or skipped questions.
SMS-based surveys allow questions to be sent to participants via SMS messaging.	Cost-effective and easy to implement. Enables participants to give honest responses to sensitive questions. Incentives can be used to increase response rates (offering airtime in return for completing a survey). Can be completed when convenient or safe for respondent. Allows mainly for closed-ended questions, but some open-ended questions can also be posed.	Requires respondents to have access to a mobile phone. Potential literacy bias. Surveys should not be longer than 15 questions. Data are of lower quality than those produced through other survey methods.
Remote sensing: geospatial technology		
Various types of **sensors** can be used to collect data regarding the frequency of predictable events. For example, sanitation sensors can be used to measure usage patterns of toilet facilities, and heat sensors can be used to measure cooking stove usage. For more information, see page 48.	Avoids bias of self-reporting. Good for reporting patterns of change. The data collection location can be recorded through use of a GPS, and results can be used to visualize information on maps.	Cost of implementing is high. Privacy concerns need to be managed before sensors are utilized.

Description	Pros	Cons
Story-based methods		
Story-gathering/completion tools can be administered remotely and are used to make sense of what happens in organizations and communities. Stories can be related to personal experiences, observations and situations. Participants can be asked to give a story on a given theme or a change, or they can be asked to complete a story. Story completions can be analysed to understand perceptions, etc., concerning the story topic (Smith 2019). A regular online survey tool, as discussed above, could be used for story gathering/completion; SPROCKLER and Sensemaker are online tools specialized for this purpose. For more information, see page 44.	Stories can be used as qualitative and quantitative data. Relevant stories can be collected (e.g. safety in a production plant, women's role in conflict resolution in communities). This methods allows for a much deeper understanding of complex social dynamics within a particular situation as compared with other data collection methods.	People need to give meaning to their own story, rather than evaluators interpreting what a story "means". Requires participants to have access to the Internet and connectivity, which increases the risk of selection bias.
Social media		
The increased use of Internet-based applications worldwide has increased the potential sources of data for evaluations. The three biggest social media platforms are described below by way of example. Using a secret **Facebook** group as a method of co-production or as a workshop in the evaluation process is feasible and acceptable. Social media hold significant potential for co-production and involvement in evaluation for populations that are geographically dispersed, time-constrained or are in other circumstances where in-person meetings are either not appropriate or not possible (Buelo, Kirk and Jepson 2020). **Twitter** data can be used in sentiment analysis, key phrase extraction and social network analysis. For guidelines on Twitter data collection, see Oxfam (2019). As one of the most prevalent mobile messaging applications worldwide, **WhatsApp** can be used to capture social behaviour in everyday life contexts and explore situations and experiences of media use in dialogue with participants. Methods can involve mobile instant messaging interviews through diaries and mobile experience sampling (Kaufmann and Peil 2019). Qualitative data from WhatsApp can be used to gather complex and personal stories from within a context. For an example of using a WhatsApp survey in an FCV context, see UNDP (2018).	Using social media can be a complementary method to inform a survey, gather and analyse reactions. The use of popular mobile applications such as WhatsApp enables a greater reach to stakeholders. Option of sending voice messages ensures inclusion of those who are illiterate.	Risks exclusion of those who do not have Internet access or the technology to access these social media. May exclude women in societies with strict gender norms.

Figure 5.2 **Use of SPROCKLER visualizer in a Pakistan gender programme**

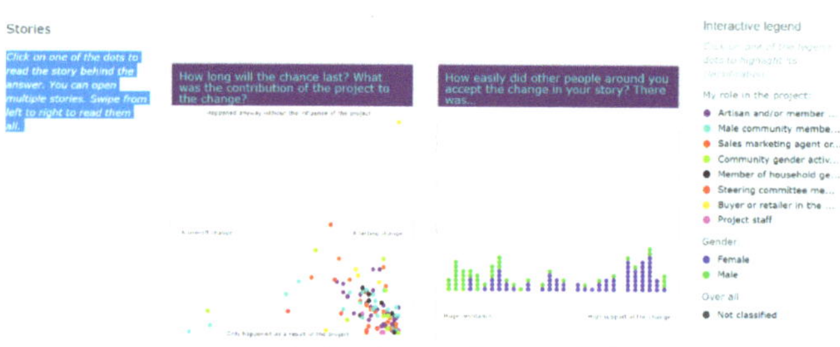

Source: SPROCKLER website, https://visualizer.sprockler.com/en/open/YCareInternationalPakistan.

Quantifiable data are gathered that capture meaning, feelings and motivations in the context shared.

Figure 5.2 shows a screen shot of the SPROCKLER visualizer in which every dot presented is a real-life story collected through an evaluation conducted in Pakistan. The graph on the right shows that for a gender equality project in rural Sindh, men faced more resistance to change compared to their counterparts. This perception was verified through a validation workshop in selected villages. The evaluators found that, due to the increased mobility of women, these men were bullied by their friends and acquaintances from neighbouring villages (Hassnain 2018).

Remote sensing: Geospatial data

At any given time, there are several thousand satellites in space collecting a vast amount of data on changes that occur on earth. These data have been widely used to understand different systems on earth; however, because there is limited guidance on how to incorporate these into an evaluation (Lech et al. 2018), satellite data and spatial methods have not been used to their full potential.

By way of example, an analysis of data from the National Aeronautics and Space Administration's Visible Infrared Imaging Radiometer Suite (NASA VIIRS) for Aleppo, Syria – a city that has been an active battle zone since 2011 – shows how satellite data can be used to derive contextual information in an FCV setting. Specifically, Aleppo's night-time radiance data show a sudden drop in brightness value around 2012, and the brightness level has been low since. Home to 2 million people before the war, the city's average radiance dropped by 85 per cent between 2011 and 2014. During the same time period, the brightness levels in towns in neighbouring Turkey remained relatively unaffected.

In addition to providing contextual information, remote sensing can be leveraged to monitor, supervise and assess results in hard-to-reach, fragile and isolated areas. Satellite remote sensing–derived indicators and proxy indicators are particularly useful in collecting time-series data on land cover changes, water quality and quantity, natural disasters, crop detection and agricultural yield estimation, pollution levels, economic activities and urbanization. Satellite-derived indicators can also be used to track illegal activities – and even migration.

For example, night-time light data acquired by NASA VIIRS are an effective proxy indicator for monitoring electricity, urbanization and economic activity. Night-time satellite data were recently used to examine the effectiveness of an electrification project in Sierra Leone (figure 5.3).

Figure 5.3 **Use of Earth observation in FCV contexts**

a. Night-time lights data for Sierra Leone, 2012 (left) and 2019 (right). Freetown is in the upper-left corner, and the Bo District is in the lower right.

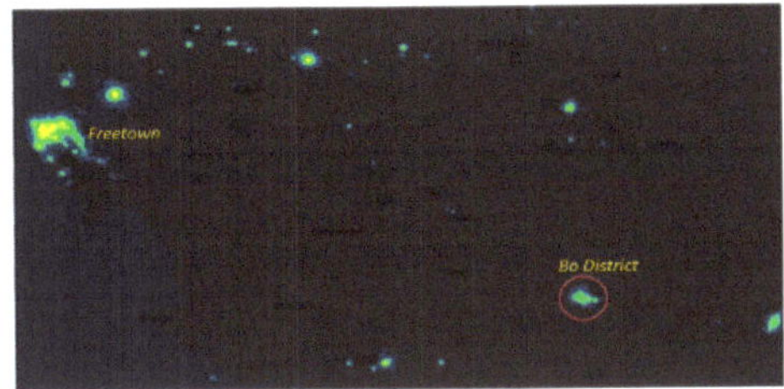

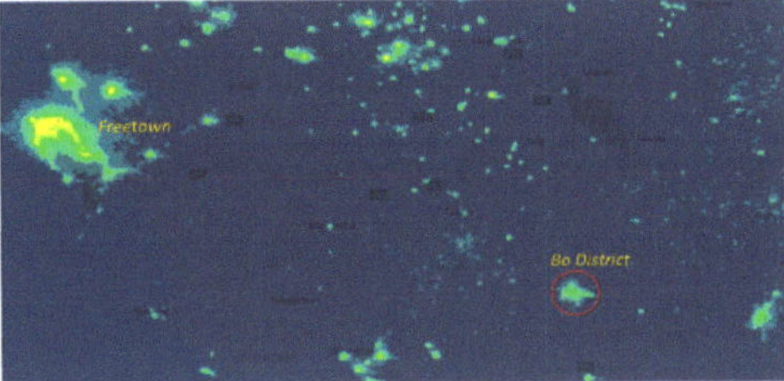

b. Times-series of light intensity at the project site. The red line shows the time of implementation of solar-based electrification.

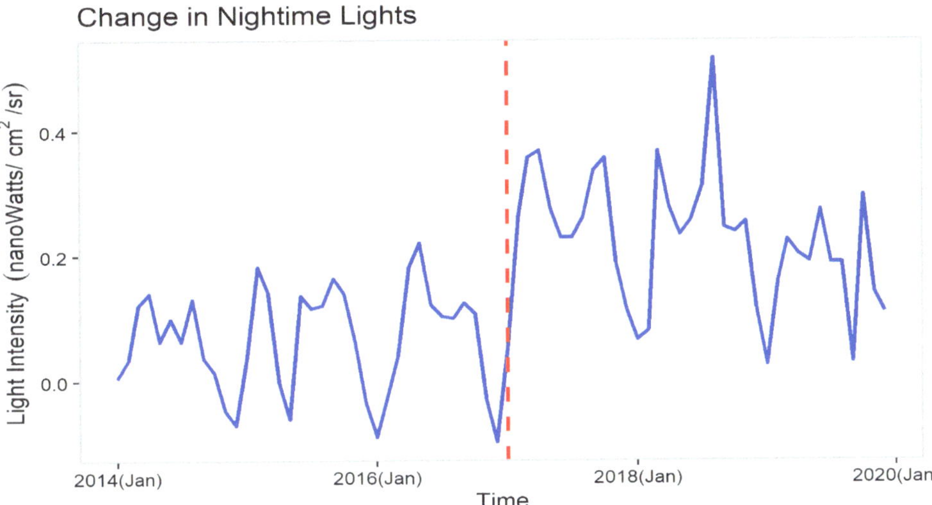

Source: Data from NASA VIIRS; Anand and Hassnain 2020.

The Rural Renewable Energy Project is an electrification intervention funded by the UK Foreign, Commonwealth and Development Office and implemented by the United Nations Office for Project Services to support the Government of Sierra Leone's goal of universal access to electricity in accordance with Sustainable Development Goal 7. The project aims to provide access to off-grid solar electricity to up to 94 communities in the country, specifically targeting community health centres to store vaccines and provide health services. Only 2.5 per cent of the rural population in Sierra Leone have access to electricity.

Reaching the selected communities for the intervention is challenging, due to the country's poor road infrastructure. Although satellite data analysis cannot completely replace conventional ways of conducting evaluations to answer effectiveness questions or capture community perceptions, it can be very useful in real-time monitoring, evaluating in FCV or pandemic situations, and/or when time and financial resources are lacking (Anand and Hassnain 2020).

Figure 5.3a shows night-time data for Sierra Leone for 2012 and 2019. An expansion of light intensity can be observed around Freetown with a relatively insignificant increase in other parts of the country. The analysis of nightlight trends for the Bumpeh Community Health Centre (figure 5.3b) shows an increase in ambient light, indicating the effectiveness of the electrification project.

The results from the analysis of night-time data were confirmed through telephone interviews with local contacts. This example highlights how remote sensing data can be used as objective evidence that helps triangulate findings obtained through other methods.

Figure 5.4 **The five As of technology access**

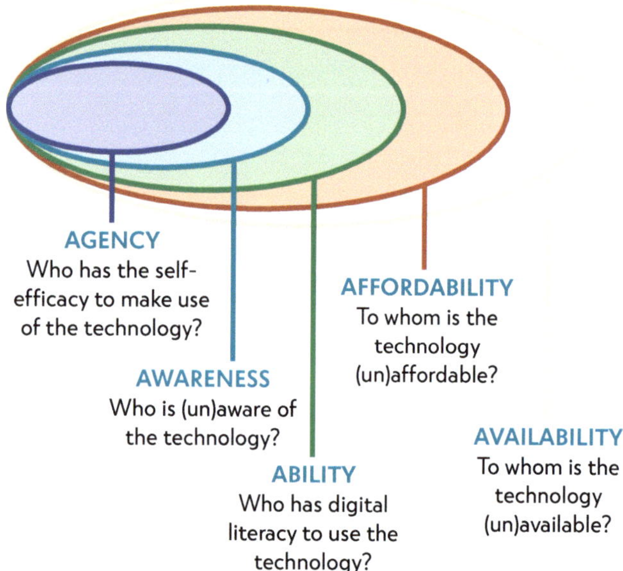

Source: Roberts and Hernandez 2019.

SELECTING THE APPROPRIATE TOOLS

When deciding on whether to use ICT tools and which to use, it may be helpful to consider the five "A" dimensions: availability, affordability, awareness, ability and agency (figure 5.4). Rather than only viewing access to technology in a binary way – e.g. those who are connected versus those who are not – these five terms provide a way to unpack other dimensions at play, including political and social factors, that may be a barrier to technology access. Structuring the analysis around these five dimensions helps decentralize the technology and highlights the social and political factors that can limit technology access (Roberts and Hernandez 2019).

TIPS FOR COLLECTING DATA USING ICTS IN FCV SETTINGS

- ICTs should not replace face-to-face contact but complement it by using and promoting mixed/appropriate method approaches.
- If ICTs are suitable for the context, be sure to select the right ones based on consideration of the sociocultural, political and technological environment and the ICTs' feasibility.
- Conduct a risk assessment and consider unintended consequences. Is anyone being put at risk? Are the potential benefits worth the risks? Identify potential unintended consequences that could result from the introduction or use of ICTs, including domestic violence against women, theft and harassment from authorities. Understand the nature of the context. How is technology seen in the community for women and for men? What restrictions may there be on women to use the

technology? Would women's participation put them at greater risk of gender-based violence?

- Train the enumerators in conflict and gender sensitivity, and make sure they understand the purpose of the data collection – especially using ICTs.
- Get feedback from enumerators and partners after data collection and involve them in analysis of the data.
- Include the community and interviewees in the process so people know why the data are being gathered. Be aware of different levels of access and inclusion, because marginalized members of a community or group may be left out if ICT-enabled monitoring and evaluation is not designed for inclusion. Build local capacity.
- Leverage earth observation data to understand the context in hard-to-reach areas. In FCV contexts, earth observation analytics can be used in planning the evaluation as well as in evaluating outcomes.
- Invest time in creating an environment of trust before and during data collection to avoid any problems or biased answers. This can be done by raising awareness among communities about why the data are being collected and how the data will be used. If using ICTs, inform people about how and why the technologies will be used in gathering data.
- Study the privacy policies of mobile service providers, and government data collection and storage regulations. When speaking to respondents, always obtain informed consent, and only collect personal information when necessary. Make sure the mobile device used has appropriate security and privacy features.
- Although ICTs can offer some options for enhanced protection such as password protection, encryption or panic buttons to delete data, be careful to navigate local laws and the context, being conscious of risks.
- Back-up solutions are important. If someone does not want their information on a machine, make sure paper can be reverted to if needed. Make sure data can be collected off-line in case there is no connection (this is often the case in FCV contexts).
- Triangulate the data using participatory and mixed methods to avoid selection and other biases while using ICTs. Where possible, use data from other sources (e.g. national statistical offices, other agencies, donors, academia, United Nations entities, etc.) to validate the evaluation's own findings.
- Do not lose contact with beneficiaries. Close the feedback loop. Do the data make sense to them? Share results effectively with intervention participants and staff, and involve them in analysis of the data to support better decision-making and learning.

For more information, see Oxfam's 2017 "Responsible Data Management Training Pack", which was developed to help introduce the principles of responsible data management and the planning processes that can be used, and to examine how unexpected issues that arise in different contexts can be handled: https://policy-practice.oxfam.org.uk/publications/responsible-data-management-training-pack-620235

An essential reference in defining data gathering plans is the 2016 SAVE Toolkit "Technologies for Monitoring in Insecure Environments": https://www.gppi.net/2016/11/09/technologies-for-monitoring-in-insecure-environments

An empty classroom as a result of conflict in the north of Central African Republic.
Photo: Hur Hassnain

Step 6: **Close the Evaluation Learning Loop**

This step addresses a key question about evaluation that has so far not been discussed in this book. Who is really benefiting from the learning results, and should the evaluators and evaluation commissions be accountable to the respondents of the evaluation?

Given the complexity, volatility and rapidly changing nature of some FCV contexts, it is especially important to share the evaluation findings in validation workshops with intervention stakeholders before the final report is written. Ideally, stakeholders should already be familiar with the evaluation and have already been engaged in its activities preceding the data analysis and reporting stages.

The benefits of meeting with the stakeholders as a community to make sense of the evaluation's data and findings are manifold. The most important of these benefits is that it makes community members aware of what worked and what did not work in the intervention, and why and why not. This information in turn stimulates reflection on future improvements.

Discussing the past can also stimulate tensions in FCV settings; refer to the information presented in Step 1 and Step 2 about engaging with different stakeholders to mitigate such problems.

Target groups for community validation workshops should be identified and agreed upon in advance. Similarly, the products that can be used for sharing the results with the intervention participants should be identified and agreed upon in advance, keeping in mind literacy, sensitivity, time and resource constraints, and other concerns.

Key activities and considerations in designing and implementing a validation workshop with intervention participants to close the evaluation learning loop are summarized below.

- **Budget for the validation workshop in the evaluation or in the evaluation terms of reference.** The validation workshop is an important use of evaluation resources. Given the low literacy levels in the communities of most interventions, a workshop is much more useful to intervention participants than an elaborate evaluation report.
- **Design the workshop with stakeholders.** The starting point in this design is preparation of the workshop agenda. Gather the necessary tools (flipcharts,

For more details, see Hassnain's 2018 blogpost, "Closing the Learning Loop – How to Extend the Ownership of Evaluation Findings to Project Beneficiaries?": https://www.linkedin.com/pulse/closing-learning-loop-how-extend-ownership-evaluation-hur-hassnain/

whiteboards, etc.), prepare sessions aligned to the key evaluation questions, and adapt the sessions according to participants' differences and needs (culture, language etc.). To ensure active participation, bring more energy into the room and increase productivity, use icebreakers and team-building techniques.

- **Identify a venue convenient for local people.** When selecting the area/village to host the meeting, consider the availability of local transport from neighbouring villages, the availability of a meeting space, and the interest and willingness of the community leaders.
- **Select the most relevant results to share.** It is not necessary to share all of the evaluation results. Select the most relevant findings and present them concisely. Where possible, convert interesting data into reader-friendly graphs.
- **Involve women, young people, sexual and gender minorities, and the poorest.** Encourage these particularly vulnerable and at-risk populations in the community to participate in the workshop so no one is left behind and all voices can be heard.
- **Speak their language.** To best engage everyone in the discussion, the workshop should be organized in the local language.
- **Explore impact causalities with people – what worked and what did not.** To make sense of the data gathered, ask participants to comment on the results of the evaluation to gain a better understanding of the causalities of impact.

PHASE C

Using the Evaluation

Children playing marbles in an activity-based evaluation exercise in Afghanistan.
Photo: Hur Hassnain

Step 7: **Report, Disseminate and Use**

Last but most definitely not least, this final step of the evaluation process is crucial to ensure that the key lessons and recommendations emerging from the evaluation are shared with relevant audiences. As with all previous steps, in contexts of fragility, conflict and violence (FCV), reporting and dissemination plans need to be adapted to ensure safety and conflict sensitivity. Budget and time constraints can mean that evaluation dissemination is not prioritized; however, actions taken to share results can be beneficial, ensuring that learning is shared not only within the organization conducting and/or commissioning the evaluation but also externally with the affected populations and other stakeholders, including the wider evaluation community.

REPORTING

Reporting in contexts of FCV entails certain challenges. Keep the following tips and techniques in mind when reporting on the evaluation and its findings.

- **Consider what is safe to share.** Be careful when communicating any information regarding the conflict's actors, profile, causes and dynamics in your reporting. Always remember **what is safe today may not be safe tomorrow**. Actors and factors, including threats and relationships, can change. Related to this, what is safe for the evaluator may not be safe for national partners or stakeholders – and vice versa. Continuous monitoring, especially of the external political environment, is critical. Communication with people who have knowledge of the context, including field-level evaluation stakeholders, can help you keep up to date with any changing social or political factors that could increase the potential risk of sharing information.
- **Report in a conflict-sensitive manner.** Integrate the evaluation findings and recommendations resulting from the analysis of the intervention into regular reporting processes. Determine the type and sensitivity of information to be included in reports by referencing the initial conflict analysis. In all cases, sensitive handling (of privacy, anonymity, etc.) should be explicitly agreed upon at the start of the evaluation process and reinforced at the reporting stage.
- **Be comprehensive.** The more insightful and comprehensive the analysis and reporting, the more influential it can be. Ensure that information is obtained from and analysed across multiple sources in the FCV context.

Present and discuss politically conflicting data/analysis from external sources in workshops. In this way, third-party opinions can be obtained, avoiding attribution to staff and partners.

- **Protect data sources.** All responses received in FCV contexts should be seen as high risk, and any source of identification should be removed. Thus, in communicating results, be sure to obscure or change names, ethnicities, religious and political affiliations, and geographic locations related to information and respondents. The World Food Programme, for instance, does not name beneficiaries or community members interviewed, instead referencing them collectively as, for example, "focus group discussion conducted with 15 female community members".
- **Ensure peer review.** Consulting other evaluation specialists for feedback on the written report is good practice to ensure quality control. Before submitting reports to donors or for publication, all evaluations should be peer reviewed.

The recommendations and conclusions of the evaluation should be responded to systematically. The people or institutions targeted by each recommendation should respond and take relevant action. The written management response – undertaken to disseminate findings and lessons, and to engage in a learning process – is the responsibility of the commissioning agency (OECD 2012).

DISSEMINATION

Disseminating the evaluation findings, along with a formal management response, to relevant stakeholders is an important step. Where possible, the findings should be made available online; this increases transparency, improves accessibility and contributes to the global knowledge base that can be accessed by external actors working in this sector. Target groups for dissemination should be agreed upon at the beginning of the process, taking into full account the confidentiality and safety of all evaluation respondents and participants.

Funds should be made available in evaluation budgets, and dissemination activities should be incorporated in the evaluation terms of reference. To the extent possible, independent national evaluators who have been part of the evaluation team should present the findings and recommendations to the affected population consulted, relevant national authorities and other in-country stakeholders. Other stakeholders, as relevant, may also be involved in disseminating the results (IAHE 2014).

For example, see the Asian Development Bank's "just-in-time" evaluation lessons responding to the COVID-19 pandemic: https://www.adb.org/site/evaluation/evaluations/covid-19-response

For wider dissemination to various public audiences, readily accessible, user-friendly materials – created for print or web distribution – such as evaluation summaries, podcasts, policy briefs, video clips, infographics and other tailored communication tools could be produced. Lessons learned documents can be particularly useful resources in fragile contexts and during crisis.

Sharing the outcomes of an evaluation can be difficult when the results are perceived as negative or when they question strategies or approaches to which practitioners feel strongly committed. Stakeholders may resist questioning the effectiveness of their approach. Receptivity can be enhanced by emphasizing the learning aspects of evaluation and by engaging stakeholders early on (OECD 2012).

See Step 1 for stakeholder engagement strategies.

Communicating evaluation findings in a format that will encourage people to read them and take action is crucial. Consider the following when planning dissemination of evaluation findings.

Define the purpose for sharing the evaluation findings.

- What do you hope to achieve?
- What action(s) do you expect to be taken?

Decide on the target audience.

- Who needs to be informed of the results (for accountability/learning purposes)?
- What kind of information do they need and why?
- How do they engage with information? Consider digital literacy levels and whether face-to-face, text, visual or spoken communication would be preferable.
- Are there any accessibility needs to consider (e.g. visual or hearing impairments)?

Translation of the evaluation findings. Effective knowledge brokering requires using innovative and creative ways to present evidence and drive evidence use.

- What data/findings best support the key messages?
- How can they be communicated in a way that is understandable to the target audience?

Decide on the most relevant format(s) for dissemination. Once you have identified the target audience, review the different available products, as listed in table 7.1, and determine the format(s) that is the most suitable overall for dissemination. See figures 7.1 and 7.2 for further guidance in dissemination product selection.

For useful links and guides on how to produce the materials listed in table 7.1, see the National Council for Voluntary Organisations webpage, "How to Use Creative Reporting Formats for Evaluation": https://knowhow.ncvo.org.uk/how-to/how-to-use-creative-reporting-formats-for-evaluation

Decide on the key messages to share with the audience.

- Depending on the product selected as most relevant for the target audience, there may be limitations on how much detail can be included. For example, focusing on the top 5 or 10 highlights of the evaluation findings will best suit most visual/spoken/interactive formats.
- Answer this question: If the audience can take away only one or two key messages, what should these be?

Use online resources to support your communication planning. There are many resources that can be accessed to help in communication planning. For example, the European Commission has produced an interactive guide for evaluation dissemination

Table 7.1 **Dissemination product options**

Type	Description	Example
Visual	Using a visual format is an excellent way to communicate a lot of information in a small space. Some visual presentations can also be included in written reports, summaries, blogs or presentations.	▪ Infographics ▪ Illustrations and cartoons ▪ Data dashboards ▪ Posters ▪ Photographs
Spoken	Using a spoken format presentation provides opportunities to hear the actual voices of evaluation participants. It is also an engaging and interactive way to communicate findings.	▪ Presentations ▪ Podcasts ▪ Videos ▪ Music, spoken word (or even interpretive dance)
Written	In addition to traditional evaluation reports, consider using shorter, more action-oriented formats.	▪ Summary reports ▪ Blogs ▪ Newsletters ▪ Postcards

Figure 7.1 **Comparing knowledge products**

CHARACTERISTICS	VIDEO	PODCASTS	INFO-GRAPHICS	BRIEFS	BLOGS
Time required	1-12 weeks	1 week	2 weeks (av.)	Variable	1-2 weeks
Expertise	In-house/ video expert	In-house/ comms expert	In-house/ comms expert	In-house/ comms expert	In-house/ comms expert
Length	3-15'	3-30'	2-4 pages	2-4 pages	1-1,500 words
Cost	€2-15,000	€600 (av.)	Max. €2,500	Max. €1,000	In-house prod.

Source: Hassnain and Mantovan 2020.

Figure 7.2 **Selecting appropriate dissemination products**

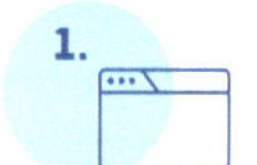

1. Browse the products
- Evaluation videos
- Evaluation briefs
- Evaluation infographics
- Evaluation podcasts
- Evaluation blogs
- Other

2. Choose your target audience
- Who is your target audience?
- What format is best to reach your audience?

3. Define key message/s
- What do you want to communicate?
- How do you want the evaluation results to be used?

4. Choose your product/s
- Which format is the most suitable overall?
- Will you have more than one product?

5. Resources
- Consider how long it takes to develop each product
- Consider additional technical skills required
- Think about potential costs involved

6. Create
- Follow the tips provided in the 'How-to' guidelines
- Remember to share your ideas with colleagues for feedback

Source: Hassnain and Mantovan 2020.

(Hassnain and Mantovan 2020) that delineates the steps to take when using blogs, videos, podcasts, briefs and infographics (see figure 7.3) to communicate evaluation results. In addition, the guide provides a list of pros and cons for each product, links to online references and a selection of good examples (see figure 7.4) of evaluation dissemination that can be used for inspiration.

Contribute to the global knowledge base for evidence produced in contexts of FCV. Final evaluation reports and related products can be published here:

- Participating agencies' websites
- Active Learning Network for Accountability and Performance (ALNAP)
- European Commission, Capacity4Dev website
- Inter-Agency Standing Committee
- ReliefWeb
- United Nations Evaluation Group
- United Nations Office for the Coordination of Humanitarian Affairs

UTILIZATION: INTERVENTION IMPROVEMENT AND LEARNING

A completed evaluation should feed back into the early stages of planning and intervention design and help address challenges by providing more evidence on the validity (or not) of the theories of change and data for comparison and reference. Evaluations carried out while an intervention is still ongoing can be used to adjust or redesign it (OECD 2012).

The final report and communication and dissemination products discussed above could be examined periodically through meta-analysis to further build a national, regional and global evidence base. Follow-up events on the key action points of the management response would also help ensure better utilization and uptake of the evaluation findings.

Figure 7.3 **Steps in using infographics for evaluation knowledge dissemination**

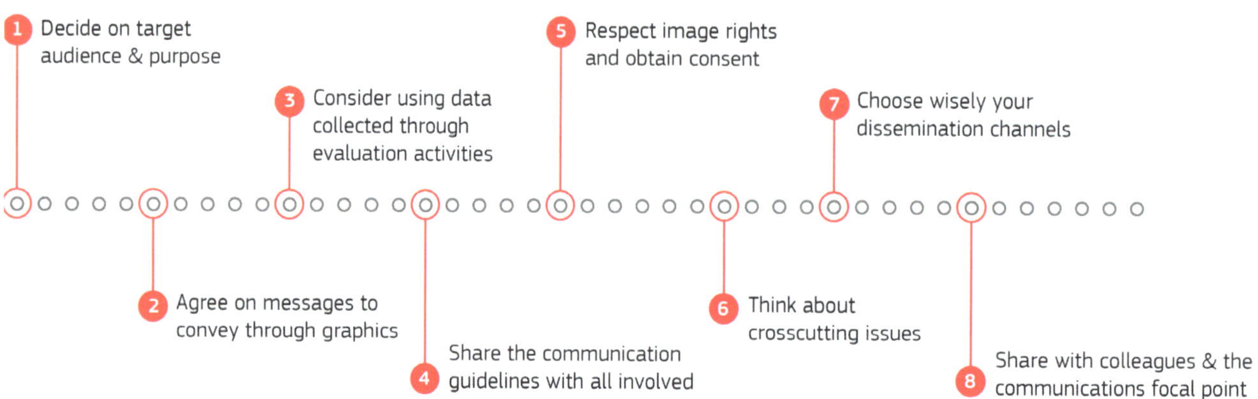

Source: Hassnain and Mantovan 2020.

Figure 7.4 **Good examples of selected evaluation dissemination products presented in interactive guide**

VIDEO

EU DELEGATION TO CÔTE D'IVOIRE

L'UE soutient le transport routier

- Description: evaluation of the Road Preservation Project in Côte d'Ivoire
- Cost of production: €15.000
- Duration: two versions (3' 15')
- Time of production: 3 months
- Produced by: contractor and local expertise

INTERNATIONAL FUND FOR AGRICULTURAL DEVELOPMENT

Strategy & Programme Evaluations

- Description: highlights from Nicaragua Country Strategy and Programme Evaluation
- Cost of production: produced in-house
- Duration: 5'38"
- Time of production: depending on scope and video length
- Produced by: IFAD headquarters

AFRICAN DEVELOPMENT BANK

AfDB support to Agricultural Value Chain Development

- Description: this video is about IDEV's evaluation of AfDB's support for agricultural value chains development in Africa
- Cost of production: +/- €10.000
- Duration: 12'22"
- Time of production: 3 weeks
- Produced by: internally

BLOGS

DG DEVCO/ESS

Evaluation from Space

- Description: how satellite data can be used for remote evaluations with an example of a UNOPS rural electrification project in Sierra Leone.
- Cost: free
- Time of production: 2 days
- Produced by: DEVCO ESS team & GEF IEO

Green Climate Fund

Country ownership in times of international assistance

- Description: showcase of the findings. It was featured in The Korea Herald, which is the biggest English language daily newspaper in the country
- Cost: free
- Time of production: 4 weeks
- Produced by: headquarters
- Language: English

IEG World Bank Group

Creating markets: A special challenge for low-income countries

- Description: how tight government fiscal positions in low-income countries justify the search for private sector solutions
- Cost: free
- Time of production: not available
- Produced by: internally
- Language: English

Source: Hassnain and Mantovan 2020.

Appendix: **Key Concepts**

This appendix defines those concepts most relevant to evaluation in FCV contexts of fragility, conflict and violence; it is by no means comprehensive.

Capacity building. Ability to transfer, improve and maintain a knowledge and resource capital. It is difficult to measure and might have unintended consequences. Also see capacity development.

Capacity development. The process through which individuals, organizations and societies obtain, strengthen and maintain the capacities to set and achieve their own development objectives over time.

Conflict. The clash of competitive actions of incompatibles that creates an antagonistic state of mind, which could lead to violence and war. Conflict per se is not necessarily bad, if controllable. The level and form of conflict is determined by the nature of the violence entailed, the number of fatalities, and the actors involved and their level of organization. International humanitarian law distinguishes between international armed conflicts between states using armed forces, and non-international armed conflict where hostilities reach "a minimum level of intensity" and parties demonstrate "a minimum" level of organization (OECD 2016). Also see conflict sensitivity.

Conflict prevention. Measures taken to try and prevent violent confrontation.

Conflict reduction. Strategies implemented with the intent of diffusing tensions and building sustainable peace.

Conflict resolution. An agreement between parties that has been prepared through negotiation to find a peaceful solution to disagreements and conflicts. The resolution should strive to be reasonable to all parties (inclusive). However, a resolution could create new conflicts.

Conflict-sensitive evaluation. Incorporates a detailed understanding of the context in terms of historical, actual or potential conflict into traditional evaluation activities and its dissemination. Conflict-sensitive evaluations are used to understand the overall impact a given intervention has had on the context and that the context has had on the intervention (International Alert et al. 2004).

Conflict sensitivity. Ability of an organization to understand the context in which it is operating, particularly the triggers and their mitigation; understand the interaction between an intervention and the context; and act on this understanding to avoid negative impacts and maximize positive impacts (International Alert et al. 2004).

Coping strategies. Is the ability of a society to bounce back after disaster? The concept is known since at least the 1970s.

Corruption. The abuse of money and trust to gain advantage for personal reasons.

Development-forced displacement and resettlement. When people are involuntarily displaced and resettled due to development interventions and climate change; see displacement and resettlement.

Disaster. Disasters can be either natural or manufactured by humans. The conjuncture of people's activities and the destructive agent constitute the "disaster". Natural disasters are related to a physical event such as flooding, earthquake, tsunami, etc. Manufactured disasters are related to war, conflicts and large infrastructural interventions such as mining, dam building and windmills.

Disaster risk reduction. A systematic approach to reduce risks and damage and prevent future catastrophes associated with disaster. The impact on society of a disaster depends on local preparedness and coping strategies.

Displacement. Physical movement of people in response to hazards, development interventions and/or violence. Displacement can be voluntary or involuntary. There are long- and short-term effects of displacement to be considered in evaluation. Displacement and resettlement are often viewed as a single interrelated process.

Equity. The quality of impartiality and fairness, and is associated with strategies to reach an equal society. There are many operational definitions of equity, some of which are contradictory; this is a challenge for evaluation.

Equity-focused evaluation. Evaluation that takes into consideration the equity dimensions of interventions, and the context and processes for the most vulnerable in society (Bamberger and Segone 2011). Equity-focused evaluation is associated with feminist evaluation and gender-responsive evaluation, but these all differ somewhat in their methodologies, approaches and values (Nandi and Nanda 2017).

Evaluation. There are many different methods, theories and approaches to evaluation. Specific to evaluation in contexts of fragility, conflict and violence is the need for an amalgamation of domains given the implicit complexity and instability of the setting. Evaluation in such settings needs to be highly sensitive to and dependent on the context. For a general definition of evaluation, see the United Nations Evaluation Group's Norms and Standards for Evaluation (UNEG 2017).

Evaluation capacity development. Refers to several strategies that together aim at a more contextually and integrated approach to address capacity building and equate capacity building with training (Tarsilla 2017).

Evaluative thinking. Systematic, intentional and ongoing attention on how to meet expected outcomes. Evaluative thinking produces effective organizations by focusing on how results are achieved, what evidence is needed to inform future actions and how to improve future results (Patton 2013).

Fragility. Fragility is associated with instability, risk and insufficient coping capacities due to the breakdown of local, traditional and state institutions. Country settings are characterized as "fragile" when an accumulation and combination of these risks are faced, along with insufficient capacity by the state, system and/or communities to manage, absorb or mitigate the consequences (OECD 2016). This situation can lead to negative outcomes, including violence, conflict, protracted political crises and chronic underdevelopment. The Organisation for Economic Co-operation and Development's fragility framework measures risks and coping capacities along five dimensions to include societal, political, economic, environmental and security aspects (OECD 2016). Peacebuilding efforts need to be comprehensive and inclusive.

Fragility, conflict and violence (FCV) is a critical development challenge that threatens efforts to end extreme poverty. By 2030, up to two-thirds of the world's extreme poor could live in FCV settings. Conflicts also drive 80 per cent of all humanitarian needs (World Bank, "Fragility, Conflict & Violence: Overview", https://www.worldbank.org/en/topic/fragilityconflictviolence/overview#1).

Gender. The socially constructed roles associated with being male and female and the relations between women and men and girls and boys. Unlike sex, which is biologically determined, gender roles are learned and change over time and across cultures (UNEP 2016).

Gender equality. When women and men are treated equally by ensuring that they have the same rights, opportunities and responsibilities; equal access to public goods and services; and equal outcomes.

Gender norms. Sets of expectations about how people of each gender should behave, according to notions of masculinity and femininity. These are not determined by biological sex but rather are specific to particular cultures or societies, and often to particular social groups within those societies (Saferworld 2016).

Governance. Decision-making in corporate, local and national or international contexts.

Harm. The unintended harmful effects on a local culture emanating from good intentions, often based on inadequate knowledge of the local culture (Anderson 1999).

Heritage. Refers to a process by which people use the past to explain and understand their own society and identity in relationship to others with material consequences.

Human rights. A universal standard promulgated in 1948 by the United Nations in the Universal Declaration of Human Rights. Most of these rights are relevant to evaluation in fragile societies.

Impoverishment Risks and Reconstruction Model. A much-used model for dealing with the negative consequences of displacement and resettlement (Cernea 2000).

Indicator. Quantitative or qualitative ratio or index used to signal and indirectly measure the performance of an intervention over time.

Intersectionality. The idea that different identities interact with each other and cannot be understood separately from one another. Notably, gender identities are shaped by other systems of power and aspects of people's identities, such as age, marital status, class, caste, race, ethnicity, religion, sexual orientation and (dis)ability (Saferworld 2016).

Monitoring. The process of collecting and analysing information on a regular basis to check, supervise, observe critically or track/record the progress of an activity, action, programme or system towards desired outcomes. Findings from monitoring data can generate questions to be answered by evaluation through more in-depth enquiry, helping to focus and increase the utility of scarce evaluation resources

Participatory evaluation. The integration of participatory evaluation methods with systems analysis.

Protective measure. Measure taken to reduce risk.

Relative deprivation. The discrepancy between what people believe they are entitled to and what they actually can have. Examples include economic opportunities, political influence or status. Relative deprivation can to lead to frustration and, ultimately in some cases, violence.

Resettlement. Following displacement, when people have reached a new place and have to adapt. Resettlement can be voluntary or involuntary. There are long- and short-term effects to be considered in evaluation. Displacement and resettlement are often viewed as a single interrelated process.

Risk. The probability of occurrence of harm and the severity of that harm.

Risk analysis. Systematic gathering and use of information/data to identify hazards and assess risk.

Risk management. Processes and structures directed towards the effective management of potential opportunities and threats.

Risk reduction. Actions aimed to lessen the probability of negative consequences associated with a particular event or series of events.

Safety. The reduction of risk to a tolerable level.

Security. A state of feeling of safety or well-being and of being protected from attack or violent conflict. The control of threat, integrated with an appropriate response capability.

Value-based evaluation: An approach based primarily, but not exclusively, on the values of the evaluand and the subject of the evaluation (Aronsson and Hassnain 2019).

Violence. The intentional use of physical force or power, threatened or actual, against oneself, another person, or against a group or community, that either results in or has a high likelihood of resulting in injury, death, psychological harm, maldevelopment or deprivation (WHO 1996).

References

ALNAP (Active Learning Network for Accountability and Performance). 2016. *Evaluating humanitarian action*. London: ALNAP. https://www.alnap.org/system/files/content/resource/files/main/alnap-evaluation-humanitarian-action-2016.pdf

ALNAP (Active Learning Network for Accountability and Performance). 2018. Evaluation of protection in humanitarian action. London: ALNAP. https://www.alnap.org/help-library/alnap-guide-evaluation-of-protection-in-humanitarian-action

Anand, A., and H. Hassnain. 2020. Evaluation from space observation. Capacity4dev, European Commission. https://europa.eu/capacity4dev/devco-ess/news/evalcrisis-blog-no-02-evaluation-space

Anderson, M. 1999. *Do no harm: how aid can support peace – or war*. Boulder: Lynne Rienner.

Aronsson, I.-L., and H. Hassnain. 2019. Value-based evaluations for transformative change. In: *Evaluation for transformational change. Opportunities and challenges for the Sustainable Development Goals*, (eds.) R. D. van den Berg, C. Magro and S. Salinas Mulder, 89–104. Exeter, UK: IDEAS.

Bamberger, M., and M. Segone. 2011. *How to design and manage equity-focused evaluations*. New York: UNICEF. https://evalpartners.org/sites/default/files/EWP5_Equity_focused_evaluations.pdf

Blommestein, N., et al. 2018. Improving financial resilience and promoting gender equality in Umerkot, Pakistan. Final evaluation report. Y Care International.

BMZ, GIZ and KfW (Federal Ministry for Economic Cooperation and Development, Deutsche Gesellschaft für Internationale Zusammenarbeit and KfW). 2014. Peace and conflict assessment: Factsheet on the "Peace and Conflict Assessment (PCA)" methodological framework.

Brown, G.K., and A. Langer (eds). 2012. *Elgar handbook of civil war and fragile states*. Cheltenham, UK: Edward Elgar Publishing Limited.

Buelo, A., A. Kirk, and R. Jepson. 2020. A novel research method for workshops and co-production of knowledge: Using a secret Facebook group. *Pilot and Feasibility Studies* 6, 168. doi:10.1186/s40814-020-00711-0

CDA Collaborative. 2017. *Faith matters: A guide for the design, monitoring and evaluation of inter-religious peacebuilding*. https://www.cdacollaborative.org/publication/faith-matters-guide-design-monitoring-evaluation-inter-religious-action-peacebuilding/

Cernea, M.M. 2000. Impoverishment risks and reconstruction: A model for population displacement and resettlement. In: *Risks and Reconstruction. Experiences of Resettlers and Refugees*, (eds.) M.M. Cernea and C. McDowell, 127–143. Washington, DC: World Bank.

Chelsky, J., and L. Kelly. 2020. Bowling in the dark: Monitoring and evaluation during COVID-19 (Coronavirus). Blogpost 1 April 2020, World Bank. https://ieg.worldbankgroup.org/blog/mande-covid19

Cockburn, C. 2010. Gender relations as causal in militarization and war. *International Feminist Journal of Politics* 12 (2): 139–157. doi: 10.1080/14616741003665169

Copes, H., W. Tchoula, F. Brookman et al. 2018. Photo-elicitation interviews with vulnerable populations: Practical and ethical considerations. *Deviant Behavior* 39 (4): 475–494.

Corral, P., A. Irwin, N. Krishnan et al. 2020. *On the front lines of the fight against poverty.* Washington, DC: World Bank Group.

Daniels, N., Gillen, P., Casson, K., and Wilson, I. (2019). STEER: Factors to Consider When Designing Online Focus Groups Using Audiovisual Technology in Health Research. International Journal of Qualitative Methods, 18, International Journal of Qualitative Methods, 14 November 2019, Vol.18.

Davies, R. 2013. *Planning evaluability assessments: A synthesis of the literature with recommendations.* London: Foreign, Commonwealth and Development Office. https://assets.publishing.service.gov.uk/media/57a08a0d40f0b652dd000534/61141-DFIDWorkingPaper40-finalOct13.pdf

DFID (Department for International Development). n.d. Interim guidance note: Measuring and managing for results in fragile and conflict-affected states and situations. https://www.alnap.org/system/files/content/resource/files/main/interimguidancenote-managing-results-in-conflict-affected-and-fragile-states-a-stock-takeoflessonsexperienceandpractice.pdf

EBRD (European Bank for Reconstruction and Development). 2012. Evaluability: Is it relevant for EBRD. Evaluation Brief, EBRD, London. https://www.ebrd.com/downloads/about/evaluation/130214.pdf

Fan, L. 2016. Disasters, conflict, and fragility: A joint agenda. Global Facility for Disaster Reduction and Recovery. https://www.gfdrr.org/sites/default/files/documents/5.%20Discussion%20Paper%20on%20Disasters%2C%20Conflict%2C%20and%20Fragility.pdf

FCDO (Foreign, Commonwealth and Development Office). 2020. Guidance. Enhanced due diligence: Safeguarding for external partners. https://www.gov.uk/guidance/safeguarding-against-sexual-exploitation-and-abuse-and-sexual-harassment-seah-in-the-aid-sector

Flynn, R., L. Albrecht, and S. Scott. 2018. Two approaches to focus group data collection for qualitative health research: Maximizing resources and data quality. *International Journal of Qualitative Methods* 17 (1).

Forrestal, S. G., A.V. D'Angelo, and L.K. Vogel. 2015. Considerations for and lessons learned from online, synchronous focus groups. *Survey Practice* 8 (2): 1–8.

FSIN (Food Security Information Network). 2020. *2020 global report on food crises: Joint analysis for better decisions.* https://docs.wfp.org/api/documents/WFP-0000114546/download/?_ga=2.75323218.1772716290.1615412176-233784304.1615412176

Gaarder, M., and J. Annan. 2013. Impact evaluation of conflict prevention and peacebuilding interventions. Independent Evaluation Group, World Bank, Washington, DC. http://documents.worldbank.org/curated/en/445741468177842482/pdf/WPS6496.pdf

Goldwyn, R., and D. Chigas. 2013. *Monitoring and evaluating conflict sensitivity: Methodological challenges and practical solutions.* CCVRI Practice Product. Cambridge, MA: CDA.

Goodchild M. 2013. The quality of big (geo) data. *Dialogues in Human Geography* 3 (3): 280–284. https://www.researchgate.net/publication/274469692_The_quality_of_big_geodata/citations

Greenleaf, A.R., and L. Vogel. 2018. *Interactive voice response for data collection in low and middle income countries.* Toronto: Viamo.

Hassnain, H. 2018. Closing the learning loop – how to extend the ownership of evaluation findings to project beneficiaries? Blogpost 23 May 2018, LinkedIn. https://www.linkedin.com/pulse/closing-learning-loop-how-extend-ownership-evaluation-hur-hassnain/

Hassnain, H. 2019a. Prediction modelling with qualitative comparative analysis and predictive analytics using EvalC3. Video presentation. https://www.youtube.com/watch?v=MXdhOwzuEeI

Hassnain, H. 2019b. Using mobile devices in hard to reach areas. Presentation to the European Commission. https://europa.eu/capacity4dev/devco-ess/wiki/3-use-mobile-phones-and-evaluation-contexts-fragility-conflict-and-violence-ideas

Hassnain, H., and A. Mantovan. 2020. Engaging your audience: Creative communications for evaluation dissemination. European Commission, Brussels. https://europa.eu/capacity4dev/evaluation_guidelines/wiki/disseminating-evaluations

Hoogeveen, J., and U. Pape. 2020. Fragility and innovations in data collection. In: Data Collection in Fragile States, (eds.) J. Hoogeveen and U. Pape. London: Palgrave Macmillan, Cham. https://doi.org/10.1007/978-3-030-25120-8_1

Hyers, L.L. 2018. *Diary methods.* New York: Oxford University Press.

IAHE Steering Group. 2014. Inter-agency humanitarian evaluations of large scale system-wide emergencies. https://interagencystandingcommittee.org/system/files/iahe_guidelines.pdf

IEP (Institute for Economics and Peace). 2020. *COVID-19 and peace.* Sydney: IEP. https://www.economicsandpeace.org/wp-content/uploads/2020/08/COVID19-and-Peaceweb.pdf

IEP (Institute for Economics and Peace). 2017. *SDG16 progress report.* Sydney: IEP. https://reliefweb.int/sites/reliefweb.int/files/resources/SDG16-Progress-Report-2017.pdf

Independent Evaluation Office of IFAD (International Fund for Agricultural Development). 2015. *Evaluation manual.* Second edition. Rome: IFAD.

Kaufmann, K., and C. Peil. 2019. The mobile instant messaging interview (MIMI): Using WhatsApp to enhance self-reporting and explore media usage in situ. *Mobile Media and Communication.* https://doi.org/10.1177/2050157919852392

Kite, J., and P. Phongsavan. 2017. Insights for conducting real-time focus groups online using a web conferencing service. *F1000Res.* 6: 122. doi:10.12688/f1000research.10427.1.

Kopper, S., and A. Sautmann. 2020. Best practices for conducting phones surveys. Blog post 20 March 2020. J-PAL. https://www.povertyactionlab.org/blog/3-20-20/best-practices-conducting-phone-surveys

Kuji-Shikatani, K., M.J. Gallagher, R. Franz, et al. 2016. Leadership support for developmental evaluative thinking: The example of the Ontario Ministry of Education. In: *Developmental evaluation exemplars: Principles in practice*, (eds.) M. Patton, K. McKegg and N. Wehipeihana, 252–270. New York: Guilford Press.

Lech, M., J.I. Uitto, S. Harten et al. 2018. Improving international development evaluation through geospatial data and analysis. *International Journal of Geospatial and Environmental Research* 5 (2). https://dc.uwm.edu/ijger/vol5/iss2/3

Nandi, R., and R.B. Nanda 2017. Integrating feminist approaches to evaluation: Lessons learned from an Indian experience. In: *Evaluation for Agenda 2030: Providing evidence on progress and sustainability*, (eds.) R.D. van den Berg, I. Naidoo and S.D. Tamondong, 187–203. Exeter, UK: IDEAS.

OECD (Organisation for Economic Co-operation and Development). 2012. *Evaluating peacebuilding activities in settings of conflict and fragility: improving learning for results.* Paris: OECD Publishing. http://dx.doi.org/10.1787/9789264106802-en

OECD (Organisation for Economic Co-operation and Development). 2016. *States of fragility 2016: Understanding violence.* Paris: OECD Publishing. http://dx.doi.org/10.1787/9789264267213-en

OECD (Organisation for Economic Co-operation and Development). 2018. *States of fragility 2018.* Paris: OECD Publishing. https://doi.org/10.1787/9789264302075-en

OECD DAC (Organisation for Economic Co-operation and Development Development Assistance Committee) Network on Development Evaluation. 2019. *Better criteria for better evaluation: Revised evaluation criteria definitions and principles for use.* Paris: OECD Publishing. https://www.oecd.org/dac/evaluation/revised-evaluation-criteria-dec-2019.pdf

OECD DAC (Organisation for Economic Co-operation and Development Development Assistance Committee). 2010. Glossary of key terms in evaluation and results based management. https://www.oecd.org/dac/evaluation/2754804.pdf

Oxfam. 2019. Going digital: Web data collection using Twitter as an example. https://policy-practice.oxfam.org.uk/publications/going-digital-web-data-collection-using-twitter-as-an-example-620948

Patton, M. 2008. *Utilization focused evaluation* (4th ed.). Thousand Oaks, CA: SAGE Publications.

Patton, M. 2013. Making evaluation meaningful and useful. Minnesota Council on Foundations.

Patton, M. 2018. *Principles-focused evaluation: The guide.* New York: Guilford Press.

Patton, M., K. McKegg, and N. Wehipeihana. 2016. *Developmental evaluation exemplars: Principles in practice.* New York: Guilford Press.

Peersman, G. 2014. Evaluative criteria. Methodological Briefs: Impact Evaluation 3, UNICEF Office of Research, Florence.

Puri, J., A. Aladysheva, V. Iversen et al. 2015. What methods may be used in impact evaluations of humanitarian assistance?' Discussion Paper No. 8755, IZA, Bonn. http://repec.iza.org/dp8755.pdf

Raftree, L., and M. Bamberger. 2014. Emerging opportunities: Monitoring and evaluation in a tech-enabled world. Discussion paper, Rockefeller Foundation.

Roberts, T., and K. Hernandez. 2019. Digital access is not binary: The 5 'A's of technology access in the Philippines. *The Electronic Journal of Information Systems in Developing Countries*. doi: 10.1002/isd2.12084.

Rowe, W. 2017. Action learning and evaluation: A transformational approach for international development. Presentation at IDEAS Global Assembly, Guanajuato, 4–8 December 2017, Mexico.

Saferworld. 2016. *Toolkit for gender analysis of conflict.* http://www.dmeforpeace.org/peacexchange/wp-content/uploads/2016/09/SW-Gender-Analyis-of-Conflict-toolkit-final-pdf.pdf

Samman, E., P. Lucci, J. Hagen-Zanker et al. 2018. *SDG progress: Fragility, crisis and leaving no one behind.* London: Overseas Development Institute. https://www.odi.org/sites/odi.org.uk/files/resource-documents/12424.pdf

Smith, B. 2019. Some modest thoughts on story completion methods in qualitative research. *Qualitative Research in Psychology* 16 (1): 156–159.

SPA (Social Policy Association). 2009. Social Policy Association guidelines on research ethics. http://www.social-policy.org.uk/downloads/SPA_code_ethics_jan09.pdf

Tarsilla, M. 2017. From evaluation capacity building to evaluation capacity development: A paradigm shift. In: *Evaluation for Agenda 2030: Providing evidence on progress and sustainability,* (eds.) R.D. van den Berg, I. Naidoo and S.D. Tamondong, 81–102. Exeter, UK: IDEAS.

UK Government Stabilisation Unit. 2019. *Guide to MEL in stabilisation and conflict.* www.gov.uk/government/publications/monitoring-evaluation-and-learning-mel-in-conflict-and-stabilisation-settings-a-guidance-note

UNDP (United Nations Development Programme). 2018. *Below the surface: Results of a WhatsApp survey of Syrian refugees and host communities in Lebanon.* https://data2.unhcr.org/en/documents/details/67579

United Nations and World Bank. 2018. *Pathways for peace: Inclusive approaches to preventing violent conflict.* Washington, DC: World Bank. https://openknowledge.worldbank.org/handle/10986/28337

UNEG (United Nations Evaluation Group). 2017. Norms and standards for evaluation. http://www.unevaluation.org/document/detail/1914

Uvin, P. 1998. *Aiding violence: The development enterprise in Rwanda.* West Hartford: Kumarian.

WFP (World Food Programme). 2016. *Protection guidance manual.* Rome: WFP. https://docs.wfp.org/api/documents/WFP-0000013164/download/

WHO (World Health Organization). 1996. WHO global consultation on violence and health. Violence: a public health priority. Document WHO/EHA/SPI.POA.2, WHO, Geneva.

World Bank. 2017. Fragility, conflict and violence: 2017 Trust Fund report. World Bank, Washington, DC. http://documents.worldbank.org/curated/en/428511521809720471/683696272_201803110085157/additional/124547-REVISED-PUBLIC-17045-TF-Annual-Report-web-Apr17.pdf

Zürcher, C. 2017. What do we (not) know about development aid and violence? A systematic review. *World Development* 98: 506–522. http://dx.doi.org/10.1016/j.worlddev.2017.05.013

IDEAS Books

Transformational Evaluation for the Global Crises of Our Times. Rob D. van den Berg, Cristina Magro and Marie-Hélène Adrien, eds. Exeter, UK: IDEAS, 2021.

Evaluation in Contexts of Fragility, Conflict and Violence: Guidance from Global Evaluation Practitioners. Hur Hassnain, Lauren Kelly and Simona Somma, eds. Exeter, UK: IDEAS, 2021.

Evaluación para el cambio transformacional. Oportunidades y desafíos para los Objetivos de Desarrollo Sostenible. Rob D. van den Berg, Cristina Magro y Silvia Salinas Mulder, eds. Exeter, UK: IDEAS. 2021.

Evaluation for Transformational Change: Opportunities and Challenges for the Sustainable Development Goals. Rob D. van den Berg, Cristina Magro and Silvia Salinas Mulder, eds. Exeter, UK: IDEAS, 2019. https://ideas-global.org/transformational-evaluation/

Evaluation for Agenda 2030: Providing Evidence for Progress and Sustainability. Rob D. van den Berg, Indran Naidoo and Susan D. Tamondong, eds. Exeter, UK: IDEAS, 2017. https://ideas-global.org/evaluation-for-agenda-2030/

Poverty, Inequality, and Evaluation: Changing Perspectives. Ray C. Rist, Marie-Helene Boily and Frederic Martin, eds. Washington, DC: World Bank, 2015. https://tinyurl.com/ru8xewyx

Development Evaluation in Times of Turbulence: Dealing with Crises That Endanger Our Future. Ray C. Rist, Marie-Helene Boily and Frederic Martin, eds. Washington, DC: World Bank, 2013. https://tinyurl.com/4hwzhezv

Influencing Change: Building Evaluation Capacity to Strengthen Governance. Ray C. Rist, Marie-Helene Boily and Frederic Martin, eds. Washington, DC: World Bank, 2011. https://tinyurl.com/fxk3xbt5

www.ingramcontent.com/pod-product-compliance
Ingram Content Group UK Ltd.
Pitfield, Milton Keynes, MK11 3LW, UK
UKHW060107300726
14090UKWH00003B/392

* 9 7 8 1 9 9 9 9 3 2 9 5 4 *